COURAGE BEYOND THE BLINDFOLD
The Last P.O.W.S of WWII

By Walter R. Ross

Co-Author
Lucille E. Waring/Ross

GLOBAL PRESS
895 Quail Chase
Collierville, TN 38017

Copyright, 1995, by Walter R. Ross, Lenexa, Kansas. All rights reserved. No portion of this book may be reproduced in any form or by any means without permission in writing from the author.

All net proceeds of the first printing of this book will go to the 9th Bomb Group Association and the Burroughs Audubon Society of K.C.

Printed in the United States of America
Cover design by Walter R. Ross and Charles Stegner.

Library of Congress Catalog #95-076491
ISBN # 1-885353-03-0

...and Japanese Colonel Chugoku shouted to Lt. Fukui "Kill! Kill them. They are of no use to us now."[1]

9TH BOMB GROUP

B29 TINIAN ISLAND 1945

---

[1] Fukui's statement during the making of the documentary film (Genaku Shi) "Killed By the Atomic Bomb".

DEDICATION

Dedicated to my children and children's children in the hope that they will remember; and to those servicemen who did not return to tell their story.

ABOUT THE AUTHOR

Following World War II, Walter entered the insurance business and continued in that field until his retirement in 1985. He is a Chartered Life Underwriter (CLU) and past president of the KC chapter. He taught insurance at Rockhurst College.

Walter is an avid birder, having identified over 500 species in the lower 48 states, and is author of two birding guides.

In 1995, Walter is serving as national Co-Chairman of the "Truman Appreciation Committee" to honor President Truman on August 5, 1995 for his decision to drop the atomic bomb.

Walter is an Eagle Scout and a recipient of the Silver Beaver Award (B.S.A.).

ACKNOWLEDGEMENTS

This story would not have been possible without the help of dear friends, family and others, especially my beloved wife Lucille, who endured the agony of waiting to hear news from the War Department about my "missing in action" status. She also put up with the stress of my giving birth to this book. If she had not kept her diary, "Letters to Lucille" it would have been impossible to remember the events, times and places. My thanks go to the contributing members of the 9th Bombardment Group: General Henry Huglin, Commanding Officer; Herbert Hobler, President 9th Bombardment Association; Gordy Nelson and Scotty Tullock who put their lives in grave danger; Ben Nicks, Aircraft Commander for editing this manuscript; Carl Holden, Stan Levine, Marty Zapf, crew members; Vernon Irvin, Larry Smith, Michael Poprick and Bob Surbaugh for contributed material; Fern Coffin, Dorothy Moore and Eleanor Johnson for their critiques; John Olson for remembering how he moved our crew from the POW camp to repatriation; Mark Lewis, Hitachi's Director of Public Relations for supplying a history of Fukui's service; Christine Bartlett, niece of Agnes Bartlett, for vignettes of Bartlett's family background; David Manard, U.S. Air Force Museum, Dayton, Ohio, for technical information; Michael Bakich, Kansas City Planetarium, for technical information; Maurice Ashland, aircraft commander, Nip Clipper, for his story; Shigee Fukui, grandson of Nobuchi Fukui, for historical information on his grandfather; Carolynn Mosher for taking on a difficult task of typing the manuscript; to Carolyn Riddle my editor, I say "Thank You." You put it all together. My many thanks to all of you.

PREFACE

My story begins near the remains of a train station, annhilated by a recent bombing. I was one of ten captives who had just survived seven days adrift at sea in eight one-man life rafts. Our filthy flight suits were tattered from exposure to the hot sun and salt water. We'd been beaten by Japanese soldiers and civilians and were forced to lie three days on the hard ground littered with debris. Two additional captives were at the edge of death. Their P.O.W. camp at Hiroshima had been destroyed when America dropped the atomic bomb, and so they remained in hiding for two days, submerged in a cess pool. But even human excrement couldn't hide them. They were recaptured and endured terrible beatings out of immeasurable frustration. Pus ran from their ears as they laid there helplessly.

The airmen and I never doubted our lives were in immediate jeopardy. As each Japanese officer appeared, we grew closer to accepting our own death. I peered through my blindfold, saw one Japanese soldier immaculately dressed in an army jacket of dark brown. His brass buttons glittered in the waning sunshine of the late afternoon. His jacket was pulled in by a belt of lustrous brown leather with a strap over his shoulder to support his Samauri sword. As he began to walk around and among my fellow prisoners, I noticed his highly polished brown leather riding boots up to his knees. His jodhpurs were pressed to stand straight out from his body.

I felt like an animal being examined for the slaughter house. Although an army cap with a small visor partly hid his face, I imagined him to be arrogant and full of malice. His gait was like a tank devouring desert sand as he strutted about.

Darkness closed in around us, intensifying my fear so that I could not imagine another sunrise. And then, the Japanese soldier said in near-perfect English, "I will return and help you."

Laying amidst such destruction, I felt little hope. I wondered, Who was this officer? What does he want from us? Is he trying to get information by being cordial?"

He left soundlessly, and another Japanese officer stood in his place. "You will go nowhere. You are staying right here." He spoke with malice, and I knew we'd been abandoned to die.

INTRODUCTION

Two days after America dropped the atomic bomb on Hiroshima my plane was shot down into Japanese waters. We were the last Americans to be taken as Japanese prisoners of war during WWII.

Courage Beyond the Blindfold is the story of our crew and the torment we endured under Japanese anger and frustration. Their children were dying, brothers were burning from the inside out, and they had only a handful of Americans to whip or beat. Our lives hung in the balance until a Japanese officer interceded. Not even years of Army training prepared me for such personal violence, nor was I prepared for an enemy's compassion.

Prior to WWII, my experiences were limited to my family, church and Boy Scouts. I learned to do what I was told to do and do it without question. But when I was taken prisoner, I experienced intense relationships with others at a time when death lurked at the end of a samurai sword. To survive, I had to overcome the early training I received as an enlisted man and officer.

I look back with regret that I did not have a closer relationship with the enlisted men prior to the time we became P.O.W.s and I rejoice in reaching that regret. During the course of my long life, I have discovered the importance of relationships, compassion, and understanding. Today, it is my most important skill.

This is my story of learning and accepting that which I could not control.

TABLE OF CONTENTS

Dedication / About the Author 4
Acknowledgements 5
Preface 6
Introduction 8
1   An Eyewitness Account 12
          Nelson Reports
2   Japan Revisited 17
          Hiroshima/1983
3   Peace Park 20
          Peace Park Memorial
4   The Enlistment 23
          Pearl Harbor
5   The Training Period 25
          Lincoln/Alamagordo (1944)
          Holliman Air Force Base
          Assembling the Crew
          Introduction to the B-29
          Fine Tuning the Crew
          The Crash
          Farewell to Lucille
          On To Combat
6   Joining the 20th Air Force 39
          The Sad Tomato
          Life on Tinian
          Letters to Lucille
          Training Continues
7   Combat Begins 48
          First Mission / May 18, 1945
          Iwo Jima
          Thousands Saved
          Defying Aerodynamics
          Stop One
              Two
              Three
              Four
              Five
          The Hole
          The Nip Clipper

8	Last Mission/Yawata	60

        The Assault
        Pilot's Flimsy
        Take Off
        News of the Atomic Bomb
        Enola Gay Story
        Japan, August 8, 1945
        Attack on Yawata

9	Nip Clipper Takes Hit	74

        Bail Out
        Hitting the Water
        Day One (Wednesday)
        Day Two (Thursday)
        Day Three (Friday)
        Day Four (Saturday)
        Day Five (Sunday)
        Day Six (Monday)
        Day Seven (Tuesday)

Special Photograph Section 85-93

10	Taken Prisoners Of War	103

        The Capture
        Encounter with the Enemy
        Neal & Brissette
        Meeting Lt. Fukui/The Christian
        First to Enter Hiroshima
        Ujima
        Tode Headquarters

11	Life in a P.O.W. Camp	123

        Meeting Fellow P.O.W.s
        News Hungry P.O.W.s
        P.O.W. Camp
        Mercy Missions
        Neighboring P.O.W. Camp
        Warehouse
        Brothel
        Selling Liquor
        Dinner Out
        The Poem

12 Repatriation...135
    Victory in the Pacific
    First Leg Yokahama
    Okinawa Typhoon
    Debriefing
    Letterman General Hospital
    Homeward Bound

13 Reunion With Fukui...................................144
    His Story/August 7, 1983
    Fukui's Story
    Fukui's Article

14 Seeking P.O.W. Camp.............................156
    The Trip

Epilogue 160

Appendix   A. B-29 Superfortress.........................163

           B. Nose Art...165

           C. History/9th Bombardment Group........166

           D. Log of Missions................................167

           E. Atomic Bomb/Lives Saved..................168

           F. Poprik's Story...................................169

           G. 9th Bombardment Group Report........171

           H. List of Items Taken..........................172

           I. Air/Sea Rescue..................................173

CHAPTER 1

An Eyewitness Account

Nelson Reports

It was a bright clear morning. We were approaching the assembly point over southern Kyushu, Japan, and had quite easily spotted the squadron leader, Nash, and our element leader, Captain Scotty Tulloch.

The first two squadrons of our group were pretty well formed and circling the Assembly point in preparation for the departure for the Initial Point (IP) of the bomb run. I closed in on Scotty's wing in Circle X-26, and saw Lieutenant George Keller's crew in Circle X-23 coming up on Scotty's other wing.

Scotty pulled us up into our position in the 5th Bomb Squadron's formation as Nash started out on his course for the impact point. We all tried to be in position while circling over the assembly area, because we could cut inside and save gas while we were pulling up into our positions. It always amazed me how a bunch, 30 to 36 B-29s, with a wingspread of 141 feet could circle a couple of times and come out en route to the IP in a tight squadron formation. My crew noted, as we headed for the IP, that Keller's plane was falling back. Anyone who has even thought about flying a bomber on a combat mission knows the danger of falling back from the formation. Fighters look for stragglers or cripples to finish off. The main defense against fighters, especially on the bomb run is straight and level pinpoint flying, and concentration of fire power generated by a tightly flown formation. As pilot George continued to fall back, I considered it an emergency and broke radio silence to ask him what the problem was. He replied that he was losing power on one of his engines and could not keep up. Scotty, of course, overheard us. I told Scotty I was dropping back to stay with George to give him additional firepower and any other assistance. We dropped back on George's right wing, and I heard Scotty tell Nash that our Element was going in on it's own.

By this time, we were passing the IP and it was time to set up the bomb run. Tom Moore, the Bombardier on our crew had formerly been an instructor for several years. He set up a bomb run for us, and asked if I wanted to relay headings to George. About this time Scotty pulled up on George's left wing. We asked Scotty if he wanted to take over the run, and he said to keep going and he'd drop when we did. We decided to open the bomb bay doors, salvo, and close the doors and immediately get on our way to Okinawa, the closest safe base, because of the engine problem in old Circle X-23.

We were now coming to the bomb release point. From here until the Nip Clipper hit the water it probably took less than 20 or 25 minutes. Things began happening so fast at this point that it seemed like ten minutes or less.

We reached the bomb release point and dropped our bombs in unison. As we started a gentle turn to the left, so that we could clear the Japanese islands and head for Okinawa, simultaneously. George reported that he was depressurizing because the bomb bay doors were stuck open.

In less than a minute, after two or three Zero type Japanese fighters had broken off their attack, I saw Circle X-23 take a direct hit by flak in the right wing between number three and four engine. Within a few seconds, the fire grew from one small flame to flames trailing behind the right wing as far back as the tail section. Smoke and flames obscured complete sight of the right blister and most of the plane. All I could see was the right wing tip, about 1/2 of the vertical fin and a little of the nose of the aircraft.

At the time of the flak hit we were over the western entrance to the Shimonoseki Straits. George started a slow, wide spiral to the left. Scotty Tulloch and I stayed in loose formation with him. I told George to bailout. He answered that he was going to try to ditch. He was descending rapidly. I started cursing him trying to emphasize how important it was that he bail the crew out instead of trying to ditch. I told him that it would only be a pool of burning fuel if he ditched. I was doing all of the radio communication with George because Scotty's transmitter was garbled and cutting out.

As they passed through 3,000 feet, parachutes started coming out of George's plane. We stayed with the plane until it hit the water. Scotty broke off from the plane when the first parachute came out. We went to work like a sheep dog trying to round up everyone in the water, while my crew and I tried to count the chutes coming out of the plane. We counted ten chutes and one that was just starting to drag out the main chute, when this person and the plane hit the water together. There was a big splash of fire, when Circle X-23 hit the water and exploded. We saw no more sign of the last parachutist. We assumed it was the aircraft commander, since he normally would have been the last out.

At first, Scotty and I decided that he would fly just above the crew members in the water, and I would climb up to where we could make radio contact with some air-sea rescue unit. We had been told that one or several navy flying boats would be in the area of Kyushu. I finally contacted a submarine who told us that he was restricted from going within 100 miles of the survivors because of the Japanese shipping lane in the area. He told us that the Navy was operating within 50 miles of us with fighters and rescue equipment. He stated that he would try to give them the coded location of our survivors. Then we lost contact with him.

Our radio operator contacted Okinawa AF headquarters on Chi. They told us that Navy rescue did all the rescue near Kyushu and Okinawa and we did not have a radio frequency to contact them. That made us mad. They said "The Navy rescue that operated all rescue in that area had no receivers tuned to our (Army Air Corps) emergency frequencies." The more we thought about that, the madder we got.

While my crew was trying to contact potential rescuers, Scotty reported that his crew had dropped rescue equipment to the survivors. We decided to change places so we could also drop equipment.

I witnessed them coming together in one group while I was aloft trying to contact would be rescuers again. The survivors were about nine miles due north of a small island called Oki-No-Shima on our maps. It was about 35 or 40 miles west-southwest of Shimonoseki. Oki-No-Shima was a round rock about one to three blocks in diameter. It had a lighthouse on its peak, and there was a dock with what looked like two tied up speed boats. Scotty's crew and mine took turns shooting up the island and boats so that they couldn't get to the survivors before our air-sea rescue.

We were so certain that Air-Sea Rescue was going to get the survivors of the Keller crew that all we were concerned with was, "How soon?" Dissatisfied with the results we decided that one of us should get to Okinawa to see if we could light some fires under the rescue people there. We checked our fuel supplies and Scotty had more than we did, so we headed for Okinawa. We had been circling the downed crew for about an hour and a half when we left.

The flight to Okinawa was uneventful except for studying the secret approach pattern for Okinawa. The bombardier, navigator and I studied them until we had them down pat. We started the pattern with our IFF in the right mode, and called Okinawa approach control. They told us to forget the pattern, turn on the IFF Emergency mode and cut across the island to Drake Field and to call on downwind (one leg of the standard landing approach pattern).

After we secured our planes, we tried to get some wheels so that we could drive across the island to Navy

Rescue headquarters, until we met a short fellow with breeches carrying a riding crop, wearing four stars. Gen. Stillwell asked what we needed a jeep for, and we told him. In about ten minutes we had a 3/5 ton truck, with driver at our disposal, until we returned to Tinian. We left our crews in the visitor's quarters.

    I then drove over to the Navy Rescue unit. We even talked about stealing a seaplane. With the fuss we were raising, the operational officer was ordered to give us just enough petrol to get back to Tinian. They wouldn't even let one of us ride up in one of their seaplanes as they searched for Keller's crew.

    Our last attempt to get the survivors was to break into Gen. Davies' staff meeting back on Tinian. He couldn't get us our seaplane either, but he did keep us in touch with the Okinawa Air-Sea Rescue.

    Gordon Nelson, Captain
    5th Squadron, 9th Bombardment Group
    20th Air Force

CHAPTER 2

Japan Revisited

Hiroshima/1983

"Years later I stood before the Hiroshima Memorial. I knelt, placed my flowers on the altar, stepped back, stood erect and saluted, honoring American P.O.W.s who were less fortunate than I. I was the lucky one. I got out."

Tomorrow I am going to visit an old friend whom I have not seen in 38 years. He was a lieutenant in the Japanese army then. His adult life had been influenced by Christians ministering in Japan.

My friend's spiritual history begins in 1549 when Ignatius Loyola, the apostle to India, and Francis Xavier of Spain went to Japan as Christian missionaries. Along with the Portuguese, the Spanish had remarkable success with conversions. At least two hundred Jesuit churches were built and by the end of the 16th century one half to one million Japanese had converted to Christianity. In the early 1600's, the Japanene government feared that the missionaries might become agents of colonialism, executed many Japanese Christians, and expelled most that remained.

For twelve centuries Japan did not have any relationship with other nations. Occasionally, they attacked Korea, until foreigners were again permitted entry in 1868 under the Meiji Dynasty.

Immediately after Japan lifted its immigration ban, the Bartlett family from the United States began their missionary work in Japan. A second generation missionary, Samuel Bartlett (1865-1937) married Fanny Gordon, the first white baby to be born in Osaka, Japan. After his ordination in 1894 Samuel Bartlett and his wife went to Kyoto, Japan, to teach and became Dean of Religious Activities at the Doshisha University.

Dr. Bartlett's influence on one of his Japanese students was so strong that the student converted to Christianity in 1924.

The student, Nobuichi Fukui, was born in 1902 in Iwakuni-Shi, Yamaguichi-Ken, Japan to Heitaro and Fui Shi-Gemoto, who were farmers and large land owners. His father was the chief of their village. As a boy Fukui lived a privileged lifestyle, going to the best prep schools prior to getting his degree from the Department of Economics at Doshisha University near Kyoto. While attending the university, he was an exchange student at Chicago University, specializing in written conversational English. Because of this, Hitachi hired him in 1928 to direct their export division.

After completing his military service, Fukui returned to Hitachi in 1930 to participate in the development of exporting order-made goods.

In November 1942, the Japanese war office commissioned Hitachi to manufacture semi-diesel engines at a factory in the Java region, which had been seized from the Dutch. He had been promoting trade with the Soviet Union in power plant equipment and for this reason was sent to Java to oversee 6,000 local workers in the manufacture of semi-diesel engines.

After two years he returned to Japan and was drafted into the army first to serve in general headquarters of the military police in China, and then as an interpreter in Hiroshima.

He spoke and understood English fluently. He heard about the pending bombings of Japan on the radio broadcast, probably from Okinawa, but he could not convince the authorities of the pending danger. He also read leaflets that had been dropped by American bombers, warning the Japanese of the impending bombings.

His train trip back to Japan on August 6, 1945, was interrupted between Jiyajimako and Onoura when the atomic bomb exploded on Hiroshima.

CHAPTER 3

Peace Park

"In 1983 trees and flowers flourished. Streets were jammed with people, cars and trolleys. I did not see any evidence of deformity caused by the bomb. The population now neared one million."

Peace Park Memorial-Hiroshima

Lucille and I visited Hiroshima on August 6, 1983, to participate in the 38th annual memorial service for American and Japanese victims of the atomic bomb. The 38th year had a special religious significance for honoring their dead.

The only visible sign of the destruction was one partially destroyed building left standing near the Peace Park. It remained to remind the citizens of the horrors of war.

Prior to participating in the memorial services, we visited the Peace Park museum, an experience I still feel unable to describe. Except for our guide we were the only caucasian persons in the crowd. It gave me an erie feeling. One question kept popping up in my thoughts. Could they know that I had bombed several of their cities? Did I show it? Could they see me as a Bombardier responsible for releasing the bombs?

In the museum there was no mention that the citizens had been warned of the impending bombing. On the contrary, the display said, "Without warning on the

6th of August 1945 a B-29 dropped the atomic bomb on Hiroshima."

We knew this statement to be wrong. The United States had dropped leaflets over several cities warning its citizens that the bombing would be by a new and terrible bomb[2].

As we toured the museum we felt very uneasy viewing how the Japanese displayed the event. Our guide had to advise us on several occasions not to openly express our emotions concerning such events as Pearl Harbor, the Bataan Death March, Corrigidor and the treatment of American servicemen when taken prisoners.

The displays we had just witnessed at the museum, the war figures of victims of the bomb, the pictures of the aftermath, the artifacts all left their impressions on my mind.

As Lucille and I approached the Peace Park altar we saw people from all over the world working together to promote a peaceful place to live. Older persons lead very small children by the hand as they made their pilgrimage toward the memorial.

Some participants in the Peace Park ceremony wore their native clothing. Priests, monks, and those of differing religious orders carried offerings to place on the altar. A sense of reverence prevailed. Many visitors carried and played musical instruments with small hand held drums like tambourines being in predominance. People came and went freely.

Of course, anti-nuclear weapons demonstrators were there with signs protesting the use of the atomic bomb as they weaved in and out in a snake dance while large numbers of police maintained order. These demonstrators appeared to be a hostile group. We played a low profile in order not to attract attention.

When Lucille and I neared the altar of the memorial we held back and watched people express their grief. Some carried flowers. Others hand held

---

[2]Source: Beyond Courage by Dorothy Cave.

symbols and bells which they struck with a small hammer type instrument.

Most of the people were of Japanese descent. As they placed their flowers, they bowed as they backed away. They held their hands prayerfully in front of their faces as they bowed. The line seemed to never end.

As my turn came, I felt that saluting would be more in keeping with our practice of honoring someone (which I did).

Just beyond the altar, a large peace bell had been erected. A large wooden hammer hung from a rope allowing the participants to swing the six foot log back and forth in order to hit the bell with a loud resounding boom.

For those who struck the bell it became a symbol of remembrance. We took our turn as I remembered our dead.

Prior to leaving Hiroshima we watched participants place paper sacks containing a lighted candle onto the dark, black river. Moved by the river's slow current, like luminaries, they gracefully floated toward the open sea. Lucille and I joined the crowd in silence, each of us remembering those we'd lost.

CHAPTER 4

The Enlistment

Pearl Harbor

Less than two months after Japan bombed Pearl Harbor on December 7, 1941, I tried to enlisted in the Air Force on February 1, 1942, only to be turned down for medical reasons.

After corrective surgery, I enlisted again on June 13, 1942, at age 22 believing I had joined the camouflage division of the Army which had advertised for artists. However, after reaching Camp Meade I was assigned to an infantry division as a regimental sign painter with the grade of private.

Finally in November 1943, I reached my original objective to join the Air Force, when my commanding officer approved my transfer just three months after being commissioned as a second lieutenant in the infantry. The quick approval came because fewer second lieutenants had lost their lives during battles throughout the world than expected. The Army had a surplus of infantry second lieutenants who could readily be transferred to another branch. In my case it was the Air Force.

I was permitted to go through Air Force training "in grade" (maintaining my rank). Financially, this was a bonus for my bride and me, but caused lots of jealousy among the cadets going through the same training. Happily, I escaped their hazing period which I had already gone through at Officers Candidate school.

I cannot remember how long basic cadet training took, but I believe it was about six weeks. During basic, I caught on to the bed check routine. Eventually, I exchanged my cot for a place in town where I could be with Lucille.

Even though an officer, I was actually required to live on base at the bachelor officers' quarters. However, during bed check each evening, the sergeant never counted the number of beds, only whether each bed was occupied. He seemed satisfied if there was one body per bed. By turning my bed into the quartermaster, I was not missed. Eventually this caught up with us when the remaining number got too small.

Following basic training, I was assigned to bombardier school in Albuquerque, New Mexico.

Ultimately, I was assigned as bombardier with the Keller crew on the Air Force's newest airplane, the B-29 Superfortress. My transfer created another personal problem in that I outranked both pilots on my plane. Although the airplane commander was in charge during flight, I always felt he was resentful of my higher rank.

CHAPTER 5

The Training Period

Lincoln/Alamagordo (1944)
"There is a shortage of housing in Alamagordo. We suggest you do not take your dependents."
                    Transportation Dept.
                    Lincoln, Nebraska

After receiving my bombardier wings at Albuquerque, New Mexico, I was ordered on October 10, 1944, to report to the classification and routing pool at the Lincoln Air Force base with two days rail travel time and eight days delay enroute. The orders were dated September 30, 1944.

Each crewman assembled there had recently completed his specialty training, i.e. pilot, bombardier, gunners, navigator, radar operator, radio operator and crew chief. After their training, each was sent to Lincoln, Nebraska, where the crews were put together and assigned to an Air Force base for crew training. Lincoln became, as we might say, a clearing house, a place to fit the airmen into a crew.

During my stay in Lincoln, I reported each day for roll call, at which time the names of the crews to be sent out to another location were announced by the officer of the day. When my name was not called I was free for the day. Due to delays in getting B-29's delivered, this procedure went on for days. In fact, I stayed at Lincoln from October 10th to December 16, 1944. It did not take too long for my wife, Lucille, and me to see all of Lincoln, so

I enrolled in an art instruction class in oil painting at the University of Nebraska.

Holliman Air Force Base

Finally, my name came up. I received orders to report to Holliman Air Force Base in Alamagordo, New Mexico, on December 16, 1944. Lucille and I decided that she would remain in Lincoln until I located an apartment. However during our parting dinner, Lucille broke down and cried, "I'm coming with you." I would be disobeying orders to take her, but I could not bear the thought of leaving her in Lincoln, alone and so far away from her Philadelphia home.

I loved her so very much that I could not come to grips with her being so unhappy. I said, "Surely the city can handle just one more couple."

After returning to our apartment we cleared out all of our food and supplies, set them on our friend's doorstep with a note of our departure, and barely caught the train for Alamagordo.

Officers were permitted to live off base with their wives and Lucille had always been successful in getting employment near the base, which assisted us financially.

In 1944, Alamagordo, NM, was nothing more than a water stop for steam-engine trains. Housing was indeed difficult to find, but we managed to rent a screened-in front porch without shades. Dressing and undressing became a strategic and tactical adventure.

Lucille was a great trooper. She held up well to all of the inconveniences just so we could be together. These were precious moments. We guarded them closely.

Each day I kept repeating, "We'll do better tomorrow." As we walked up and down street after street, day after day, searching for an apartment, I would shout, "There's a potential one. Let's try this one."

"There's a for rent sign," she would announce. We knocked on door after door. Finally, we located a home where the landlord had rented her room to another serviceman who immediately went on a two weeks furlough. He paid two weeks in advance. "You can have his place until he returns," she said, "but you have to pay two weeks in advance." Her double renting did not sit well with us but it was better than the screened porch, and we welcomed the time to look for another place.

The room was so small we had to pull our suitcases out into the hall in order to get to our clothes. "I wonder if it's all worth it," Lucille kept saying. "It's better than being separated," I replied.

As Christmas neared we purchased a small Christmas tree. However, we could not find decorations because of government restrictions on producing only war material. So, we cut the Sunday comic strips into five inch strips and glued them together into a chain. We did find some tinsel, and created one of the most intimate Christmases we've ever known.

Assembling the Crew

The day following our arrival at Holliman Air Force base, the members of the Keller crew assembled. Strangers, we were, all of us. But as a flight crew, we knew we'd be crammed together inside a small cabin. Each of us was dependent upon the other for survival. One by one, we stepped forward and introduced ourselves. We even mentioned the location of our training, as if it might verify our specialties.

Stan Levine said he lived in Hughesville, Pennsylvania. I felt like I had found a buddy.

I said, "Do you know Eagles Mere?"

"Sure do," he replied. "I used to date the daughters of the rich snobs from Philadelphia."

"I caddied there while living at a Boy Scout camp," I answered. "Ever toboggan onto the lake by the Lakeside Hotel?"

"Hell, yes. Wasn't it great?"

Levine was a tall lanky guy, well over six feet tall and not an ounce of fat. He said, "I'm Jewish, born in Williamsport, Pennsylvania, in 1915. My parents are in the furniture business. I enlisted in January, '42, after attending the Wharton school and Penn State. Received my radar navigation wings and commission in June '44. So far, the happiest time I've had in the service was teaching military correspondence and typing to four classes of 50 girls each at Lowry field in Denver, Colorado."

Carl Holden was built like Levine, maybe even taller. He seemed polished from the first moment he spoke. "I was born in Malden, Massachusetts in 1924, attended public schools and then Northeastern University. Joined the Army Air Corps Cadet program and received my pilot wings and commission in August '44, went to advanced training in Albany, Georgia, and completed B-17 transition at Sebring, Florida. Then I signed up to come here in B-29s."

About that time, George Keller arrived. He was just the opposite of the other two, not exactly short, but portly, which tended to make him appear shorter. He was dark haired, sporting a tan that showed off his white teeth and a bright smile. He looked like a commander. He said, "Hello, men. I'm from Fort Wayne, Indiana, married to Berdella, who is with me in town and I will be your aircraft commander. I have been flying B-17s in Florida." He had a suntan to prove it.

Eugene Correll was a southern gentleman who spoke with a drawl as he made his introductions. "I'm from Concord, North Carolina, married to Angell, who is home taking care of our baby girl. I'm the new kid. Just received my navigation wings and commission."

"And I'm Walter Ross, your bombardier. I'm from Philadelphia. Before enlisting in June 1942, I was a commercial artist in a lithographing company. I thought the infantry might commission me as a regimental sign painter. I became a 90-day wonder receiving a commission in the infantry in 1943. My wife, Lucille, and I are staying in town."

At five foot seven, barely 135 pounds, I felt small compared to the others. My hair at that time was so blond that the boys called me "Whitey."

Shelby Fowler, the flight engineer came forward and introduced himself, "I was born June 29, 1915 in Oak Grove, Louisiana." When he mentioned he had been at Camp Blanding with the National Guard I jumped in,

"Camp Blanding? I was married there December 1942." But he said, "I left in July 1941 to enter the Air Force and married Dorothy in April 1942." Fowler had a lot of experiences with the B-29 before he joined us. Later I learned he was a great field goal kicker, missing only once during his high school career. He became a minister after the war.

The next guy to say hello was Christian Nikitas, a dark Greek extraction with a broad smile. He said, "I'm your tailgunner." I said, "Since I am 99 feet in front of you in the nose of the plane, I won't be seeing much of you." Everyone seemed to enjoy the remark which broke up the formality of the meeting. Nikitas said, "Call me Nick. I'm from Fitchburg, Massachusetts." Holden interrupted, "Welcome, from the bay state." I really did not see much of Nikitas after that.

The oldest one to join us was Travers Harmon, a blond with razor-short hair, from Washington, D.C. He had been married for what seemed like a long time to the rest of us. Harmon said, "I was a policeman in Washington, D.C. before joining and will be your right gunner."

The contrast in age between Martin Zapf and the others was obvious as he stepped forward. "I'm Marty, your radio operator. I'm from Princeton, New Jersey, born there in November in 1925, drafted in February 1944." He had sandy hair with a freckled face, a thin shy person at the time among all the so-called older persons. It seemed age differences were more noticeable with the younger boys. "I was trained at Greensboro, North Carolina and Scott field, Illinois." Correll seized the moment to jump in and talk about his home state of North Carolina.

Robert Conley said, "I'm from the Chicago area and will be your central fire control officer."

"What is that?" we asked, showing how little we knew about the plane. He went on, "I sit in a turret in the plane's forward compartment that rotates 360 degrees. My head looks out through a glass bubble mounted on the top of the fuselage from which I can look in all directions for enemy planes." He was another tall dark haired guy with lots of personality.

The final man to step forward was Gerald Blake from Buffalo, New York. We all asked questions about Niagara Falls. He said, "I'm your left gunner. I took my gunnery training in Las Vegas." Again, we questioned him about seeing the gambling. I said, "I was sent to that school, but they closed it and we returned to Santa Anna for a month of leave time."

As I shook hands with each of them, I remembered my drill sergeant warning me not to get too buddy-buddy with other members in the unit. "You get personal, you jeopardize your judgment, and you forget how to command. Death during combat is devastating if you lose a close buddy."

With this background I never got too close to the enlisted men in the crew. I did get to know some of the officers, but always maintained my distance. All were nice guys, but I did not want to know their background and family. To this day I have regretted this.

While in Lincoln, I had decided to grow a mustache. It didn't go over too well with the other crew members, so off it went. In addition to meeting the new crew members, I was delighted to meet an old buddy of mine, Warren Warchus. We trained together at bombardier school in Albuquerque. He brought not only his wife but their new baby boy, Lee, who became a big hit. He was cute, a beautiful baby. And the only one on base.

Introduction to the B-29

Within the next few days our newly assembled crew was introduced to the secrets of America's newest weapon of World War II, the B-29 Superfortress[3]". This was a giant step up from my Bombardier training at Albuquerque, which was limited to the ATII training plane, a small twin engine single wing plane.

Each crew member had also been trained at his individual skill. None of us had any idea how a B-29

---

[3]See appendix A page 163

worked. Now each of us were required to adjust our training and accept new positions on the Superfortress.

My first bombardier training phase was confined to classroom study, where I learned mathematics, weather, theory of how a plane flies, the bombsight, bombing techniques, mapping, and use of a compass. (My Boy Scout skills came in handy here.)

Classroom, classroom after classroom; day in day out. I was anxious to get to dropping the bombs. We also learned the effect of winds, and how they caused the plane to drift off course.

Then, I learned how to use the E6B (the forerunner of our present day computer). This handheld instrument consisted of a round metal disk with a clear face on one side. On the reverse side a portion could be rotated which contained numbers and instructions. A plastic card about 4" by 6" ran through the disk. The card had a series of lines on it visible through the clear face on which I could mark my calculations as I manipulated the plastic card up and down. The resulting drawing on the clear face was used to advise the pilot as to his heading and estimated time of arrival over the target or airport, including information I needed for dropping bombs.

To arrive at my conclusion, I inserted the wind speed, ground speed, drift and altitude of the plane.

For example, if the wind speed was 100 mph and the plane was headed directly into the wind at 300 mph then the ground speed would be reduced to 200 mph and visa versa with a tail wind.

If the wind blew toward either side of the plane it would blow the plane off course. I calculated the amount of drift adjustment by lining up a particular spot on the ground at 12 o'clock on the vertical crosshair in the bomb sight until the spot appeared to be running down the line toward 6 o'clock. I relayed the amount of drift to the pilot who in turn reset the plane's heading. I continued this procedure, dead reckoning, throughout the flight.

All this theory on the ground was later put to test in the air with one intermediate step: mastering the bombing simulator, which almost became my downfall.

My inclination toward achieving perfection continued to get in my way, almost to the point of disqualifying me as a bombardier.

The bombing simulator was a tower of about 10 feet high mounted on wheels driven by a motor, with a platform on top. A bomb sight and a seat were mounted to the platform. From the seat, I would assume to be in a plane looking down at a target on the floor. The tower moved toward the target on my command. Here is where my attempt toward perfection got in the way. My last minute changes in direction or speed threw off my aim, resulting in my missing the center of the target. My scores were nearly below the acceptable level. This fault "toward perfection" continued when I advanced to dropping bombs from the air. I barely qualified.

During the early stages of bombing from a plane, we photographed where our bombs would have hit had we been dropping bombs. As our training continued we dropped sand filled bombs on targets painted in the desert like archery bulls eyes.

Our flight training continued with a group of about six cadettes flying together, each taking turns at being either a bombardier or navigator.

We also learned some navigation. This dual training program by the Air Force took place because a bombardier could be assigned to an airplane that did not include a navigator it also prepared the bombardier to assist a navigator (if assigned on board) or to take over that duty in case the navigator was incapacitated on a mission.

Fine Tuning the Crew

The Keller crew began training the next day which honed each crew members' skills. Keller shot landings while each crew member sat at his position. In the beginning, George acted as co-pilot, with an instructor pilot acting as pilot. Then they reversed the order, with Keller shooting the landings. Hour by hour, he took off and landed the plane, again and again. In the beginning I did not have much confidence in him. After all, he had never flown a B-29 before. Some scary and bumpy moments followed. As he tried to land the plane, we hit the ground so hard we bounced high into the air, bouncing again and again during his attempted landings until he got it right. The nose of the B-29 had glass on the sides, the top and the front, and became known as the greenhouse. I sat in this greenhouse and watched the ground coming closer and closer during each attempted landing.

In case of a crash I would be the first crew member to hit the ground if the pilot misjudged his height above the runway. During his first landing, I began to sweat. My palms got wet. The nose of the plane was getting closer and closer to the ground. The black tire marks on the runway left by previous planes became more visible. I thought, "Will the instructor pilot be able to take over the controls soon enough to prevent a crash?" All of a sudden Keller decided we were too far down the runway to make a safe landing. He pulled the plane up, made a 360 degree turn, gained altitude and tried again. This only increased my fright, and now, I had to go through this one more time. I asked myself, "Did I get the best pilot? Were other crews experiencing the same situation? Will I live to ask?" This procedure continued until Keller was able to make smooth landings with the instructor on board.

The next scary moment arrived when I had to sit and observe Keller at the controls without an instructor pilot on board. It was fright time all over again.

The Crash

"I saw them. The sands, around the airport, appear to be as smooth as a beach, but it's made up of hills and deep valleys."

Lt. George Keller, Airplane Commander

Holliman Air Force base was located near White Sands. Looking down from the air the terrain looked like a perfect place for an emergency landing. It reminded me of the beaches in south New Jersey.

On Easter Sunday, Lucille and I were having breakfast in a downtown restaurant with the Warchus family. We were playing with their new baby, when we heard from the base the loudest explosion I've ever heard. There was no doubt in our minds as to what had happened as we all rushed out onto the sidewalk. Black smoke was bellowing high above the roof tops of the downtown buildings. As the smoke drifted across the sky it almost blocked out the sun. We just knew it was one of our B-29s. Panic was setting in; we were acquainted with most of the fellows. Lucille started shouting, "Why, oh why? What a horrible thing to happen, especially on Easter Sunday. I must know some of the wives of the men on board. Who is flying today?"

Waiting to get the answers seemed to take forever. The joy of Easter was over. We returned to our apartments to wait for the answers.

The day following the accident the other pilots were loaded onto open bed trucks and driven through the sandy area to see how the terrain looked from the ground. They learned it had hills and valleys with such variation as to make it impossible for a B-29 to make a safe emergency landing. This became a good classroom lesson for the pilots. I am not aware that any planes had previously crashed into this area, but following the pilot's sojourn into the sand hills, we never experienced another crash while there.

During the months that followed, each crewman had specialty training while the others looked on. My bombardering skills continued to improve. I even hit the bull's eye on several practice bombing runs. Gradually, the crew blended into a well-oiled working machine. The training program ended for crew #427 on April 12, 1945, when we received orders to go by train to Herington, Kansas. There, we would receive a new B-29 just off the assembly line for our flight overseas.

Farewell to Lucille

Stateside training from June 13, 1942, to April 12, 1945, finally came to an end for me.

The night before I left for overseas, Lucille and I had a delightful quiet dinner alone at the officer's club. We talked about our fun times together, our courtship back in Philly, the walks in nearby Cobb's Creek park and finding a place in Alamagordo. We reminisced about our wedding at Camp Blanding, Florida, and how close we'd become after our two-day honeymoon in St. Augustine.

Following dinner, we returned to our room to make love. I loved feeling close to her. At times, we cried, trying to accept the fact that the day we would have to part had come. Although I never said it, I knew this could be a long separation.

We did not sleep much that night. Each time I slipped into a dream, I reached for her and brought her closer.

At dawn, Lucille watched as I boarded the train. Slowly we pulled away from the station. I saw her crying. I tried not to weep in front of the other men, but it was hard to contain my emotions.

As the train accelerated and the distance between us increased, I suddenly realized that she would be alone until she reached Philly, except for a stop in New Orleans to have dinner with my older brother, Edgar, stationed there with the Army.

I would be with crewmen and others on board, but she would have no one. I was also excited about combat, and that would keep me occupied.

Lucille went to the east while I went west. She returned to our old neighborhood in Philadelphia to live with her aunt, and I to the Pacific.

Knowing I was heading for the Japan, I recalled an activity I loved during high school: assembling Japanese gardens in colorful bowls. I said as I made them, "I would like to visit Japan some day." At the time, this had to be my wildest dream. If only, my visit could have been under different circumstances.

On To Combat
> "Can anyone take the place of President Roosevelt?"
>
> Question by Keller crew

On our way to Herington, the crew learned of the death of President Franklin D. Roosevelt, shaky news for a crew on its way to combat. We asked ourselves, "Who is our new Commander-in-Chief? Who is Harry Truman?[4] Would he be able to lead in the shadow of Roosevelt?" (Later we would come to admire Truman as an outstanding leader who had the courage to order the dropping of the atomic bomb, a weapon of which he had no knowledge prior to becoming president.)

The next day we departed Herington for combat under a new Commander-in-Chief, an unsettling beginning.

Once again we had been advised not to take our wives to Herington, since our assignment there would be just to pick up the plane and continue on. However, Keller did take his wife Berdella. As we flew from the field we waved our good-byes to her. It was the last time she saw her husband alive.

Our first leg took us to Sacramento. The flight went as planned. What a thrill seeing the snow-capped Rockies during my first flight to the west coast. I had the best seat in the plane. This time I did not mind sitting in the greenhouse.

"Let's party. Let's go down town. Our last night stateside. Our last fling," the crew's officers shouted as we arrived at our quarters.

I collected all of their money prior to going since I was the only non-drinker. My responsibility was to pay all bills, secure the taxi and get them back to base safely and on time. What a night! I can still feel Keller's heel

---

[4]Kit Bond, Senator from Missouri, stated years later that Truman's eleven years stay at his farm in Missouri from 1906 to 1917 prior to his going into the Army in WWI played an integral role in shaping the character and values of the future President. Source: James Worsham Washington correspondent.

coming down hard on top of my foot as I helped him into the taxi. The man weighed twice as much as me, and it seemed like forever before he took his foot off mine. He was feeling no pain after a night of drinking and he wobbled unsteadily.

After an overnight stay in Sacramento, I settled up with each man and returned money to each as we flew to Hawaii. Upon landing, we received orders to stand armed guard over our plane 24 hours a day since we were now in the combat zone.

The crew, except for Stan Levine, visited Honolulu. We took in dinner at an open air restaurant with just a roof over it. The food was not too good compared to the Air Force dinners. There were many birds all around us. They even came to our table and I fed them bread. Such beggars.

When dinner was over we went sight seeing. Not only were the streets lined with beautiful coconut palm trees but it was wall to wall service personnel from all of the branches. Due to its location in the Pacific, Hawaii became the crossroads for ships and planes coming from the mainland or returning from the South Pacific. Planes refueled and ships unloaded supplies. The Army and Navy had large contingencies of personnel stationed there, battle ready since the threat of an invasion still lingered. It was also a staging area for troops going to the South Pacific and developed into a popular place for combat servicemen and women to spend their R&R (rest and relaxation).

We visited lovely Waikiki beach and watched the surfers riding the waves. Since this was our first time to witness such an event we were fascinated by their skill. Of course we did some girl watching, mostly Hawaiians dressed in their abbreviated two piece bathing suits, or long native dresses.

Our time in Honolulu was limited by the curfew, but before returning to base we visited Pearl Harbor. I could not believe my eyes, although a lot of clean up had been done, the place was still "Disasterville."

With our long trip from Sacramento and our sight seeing we were exhausted by the time we returned to base, so off to bed (cots, sheets, mattresses and blankets) at 2200 (10 p.m. civilian time). I slept until eight o'clock the next morning. I did not need blankets until early in the morning when a chill blew up. We slept in an open bay barracks on the base. Because of the heavy humidity, my clothes felt very damp when I awoke.

Upon leaving we were given secret battle orders. I purchased some cases of pineapple juice at $3.60 for 24 cans and cartons of cigarettes for $.50 each. Even though I did not smoke, they would be good for barter. I also bought some t-shirts.

As I left Hawaii I began to realize that I had reached the point of no return. We were now in the combat zone. I had just witnessed the horrors of war at Pearl Harbor and saw first hand what capabilities the enemy had. I was scared. I missed Lucille. She was the only one I could have expressed these feelings to. I had no one to turn to. We all put on a carefree attitude but it was just a facade for me. Everywhere I turned, it was men, men, men. They would not admit their feelings, nor would I.

From Hickam field we stopped on Johnston Island to refuel and then onto Kwajalein in the middle of the Pacific Ocean. During our descent, from my vantage point in the nose of the plane, I could see the water getting closer and closer, and was relieved when we hit solid land. As our plane landed, the ocean lapped onto the runway and our wheels touched water. The runway covered the entire length of the island of Kwajalein and on take off our wheels were in the ocean. After leaving Kwajalein we opened our secret orders to learn that Tinian in the Marianas would be our final destination. (Guam and Saipan are also included within this chain of islands.)

CHAPTER 6

Joining the 20th Air Force

The Sad Tomato[5]

Upon arrival on Tinian April 29, 1945, the operational officer assigned our spanking new plane to a veteran crew and replaced it with a plane named Sad Tomato.

I never met the original crew of the Sad Tomato nor did I know how it received its name. The drawing[6] on the nose of the plane consisted of the word "Sad" followed by a large red tomato. Emerging from it was a cartoon type worm holding binoculars to its eyes. It served us well most of the time but occasionally lived up to its name.

The Keller crew, named after its airplane commander, was also called the crew of the Sad Tomato. We were assigned to the 5th Squadron, 9th Bombardment[7] Group, 313th wing of the 20th Air Force as a replacement crew with Col. Henry Huglin as the commanding officer of the 9th Bombardment Group (a B-29 unit).

---

[5]The "Sad Tomato" left the United States for Tinian on 20 Jan 1945, returning to the U.S. and reclaimed (dismantled) 10 May 1954.

[6]Names and drawings (i.e. nose art, cartoons, characters, sexual or suggestive names, and cities) appeared on planes prior to combat in an attempt to humanize the brutal war. See Appendix B page 165.

[7]See Appendix C page 166.

Life On Tinian

"The stench blowing from the compound housing the natives was so bad it made me sick at the stomach."

Ten officers were housed together in a tent as temporary housing until a Quonset hut could be built for us. We broke up wooden boxes for flooring and quite fortunately located an electric refrigerator for our tent. Each day we kept our canteens in the refrigerator so we would have cool water. I kept a box of candy from Lucille in the refrigerator to prevent it from melting in this hot and humid place. I put the remaining two cans of pineapple juice purchased in Hawaii on ice for the first night's refreshments.

One of the most popular songs sung by the enlisted men on Tinian was to the tune of "Rum and Coca-Cola."

Have you ever been to Tinian?
It's Heaven for the enlisted man.
There's whisky, girls and other such.
But all are labeled: "Mustn't touch."

This tropic isle's a paradise,
Of muddy roads and rainy skies.
Outdoor latrines and fungus feet,
And every day more goat to eat.

Enlisted men are on the beam,
Officers say "We're one big team."
But do they ever share the rum and Coke?
Ha, ha, ha, that's one big joke.

To me the island of Tinian, which had many trees, seemed quite large. Years earlier the Japanese brought Korean labor to Tinian to plant sugarcane in most of the fields. As a matter of history, Japan had been imperialist rulers over Korea since the fifth century. The Japanese dictatorship divided Korea into 95 states.

When the Americans arrived they set up the island like New York City with roads and parks named after New York streets, villas, and parks. Central Park became the focal point.

I am sorry to say that we disrespectively called the inhabitants (Koreans) gooks. We would look at them and say, "Oh, you're ugly." Not understanding English they would smile and bow to us. It was a mean sport for us to do. Oddly, Koreans and Japanese had been rounded up by our military as prisoners of war and put into an area surrounded by barb wire with guards to watch over them. Each day, under guard, they were taken outside the compound to work throughout the island: cleaning it up, digging trenches, building coral walls and roads.

The Koreans were such small people, they could walk under my outstretched arms (at my height of 5'7").

Some of the Korean and Japanese prisoners worked in the officers' laundry. At first they had a difficult time learning how to operate the washing machines; later when they learned how to use the machines, they acted like kids with a new toy and did a fairly good job. As our need for dry, clean clothing exceeded the ten pieces of clothing each officer was permitted to send to the laundry each week, most of us did some washing on our own.

The big deal was for each man to build his own washing machine. Some men built machines out of a 55 gallon drum with wooden paddles inside, driven by a homemade windmill. Since the wind blew constantly, they had ongoing power. To take advantage of this wind, the windmills were all lined up on top of the cliff facing the ocean.

My washing machine was not so inventive, it was just a five gallon can that I placed on top of rocks and built a fire under it. When the water was hot I added soap, my clothes, and boiled them. After a good rinse I hung them up, hoping they would dry before the next rain came.

Our first meal on Tinian consisted of fried chicken, fried potatoes, string beans, mixed fruit and cake. We were really roughing it.

Most of our food was brought in by plane and prepared by full-time cooks and served cafeteria style in a permanent mess hall. I'm sorry to say the infantry and Marines did not enjoy this comfort. They were always on the move and carried their 'K' and 'C' rations with them. Their menu was very limited.

Whenever I watched the foot soldiers pass through our area I said to myself, "I'm glad I'm not back in the infantry." I felt blessed to have a bed to sleep in each night and a place to eat.

After dinner in the mess hall, and some sack time, we went to an all Navy show to hear band leader Claude Thornhill. While listening to the band play, I thought back to the time Lucille and I saw him at Sunnybrook ballroom, just outside of Philadelphia. That night he played "Autumn Leaves" and looked back over his shoulder at Lucille. She almost collapsed.

The memory of that evening was so powerful, I found it hard to bring myself back to this show. Lucille was constantly on my mind but suddenly, I realized just how much I missed her. We were Big Band fans. Hearing this one brought to light all the good times we had together as the bands passed through Philly. It was easy for me to drift back to those days as the band played on.

During my stay on Tinian, I saw shows like this often and enjoyed all of them. Each branch of the service had its own military band and swing orchestra to perform for us. Plus the U.S.O. brought in traveling professional shows like Bob Hope, etc. to entertain us. I gladly sat through heavy rainstorms many times just to see a show.

We continued living in our tent until the Navy Seabees put up a Quonset hut for us. When completed, I joined eleven other officers from three different crews and we all moved in together. Keller was housed with other airplane commanders. Carl Holden put together a work crew who built a front and back sitting porch. Tom Simpson, another pilot, got upset as I sprayed DDT all around the Quonset to kill the bugs. (This was before we knew about the harm it did to the environment.) Bob Crews and Carl Holden struck up a friendship since they were both from New England and interested in sailboats. My friend Warren Warchus came over for our house warming party. The Seabees, only one part of the Navy, did all of the construction work on the island along with the Army engineers.

A Quonset hut is a prefabricated structure of corrugated metal. It is like a pipe cut in half lengthwise. There were two windows on each side with a wall built at both ends with a door. The sides going toward the roof had a break in them allowing the roof to hang over the break for ventilation. This was great except during severe rain storms with heavy winds, then the rain would come in. We finally bent the overhang down to prevent the water from blowing in. I used the cigarettes purchased in Hawaii to pay the Seabees for building some shelves.

Rain was a daily occurrence on Tinian. Wash-outs were frequent and caused much misery. Our Quonset huts were greatly appreciated over the leaky tents.

Wearing wooden shoes became the style of the day, so I made a pair for myself. After locating some wood I whittled a right and left. Then I tacked pieces of canvas on one side and over to the other side as straps to hold them onto my feet. In addition to our wooden shoes we all wore shorts made by cutting off the legs of our khaki pants. Since cloth material was scarce, I turned the discarded end into a laundry bag by sewing up one end, and made a draw string at the open end.

During the time between our arrival on Tinian and our first bombing mission we had plenty of spare time.

When the officers completed building our officer's club we built a large dice table (6'x10'). Following payday a crap game went on constantly until one person had all the money. The only thing that interrupted the game was a bombing mission.

Since I never could get the hang of craps I turned to Black Jack. That became my game, and a profitable one too.

Lucille asked, "Why are you sending all these checks home signed by different officers? Where are they coming from?" In the short span that I participated I sent home about $500 (a large sum in those days).

The officers established a liquor club. Each officer who joined was permitted to receive one fifth of liquor each week. Even though I did not drink, I joined by contributing $40.00 because liquor was a good bartering commodity.

Carl Holden (co-pilot) and I used three "fifths" (bottles) to make a down payment on a motor scooter, which we purchased from the Seabees. We learned later that the Seabees came looking for their additional bottles of liquor after we were reported as "missing in action."

There were no gas stations on Tinian (all of the gas belonged to the government) so we got ours at the motor pool by draining gas, trapped in the loop of the gas tank hoses. It did not take much to fill our small tank.

After we moved into our new quarters, without telling anyone what I was doing on several occasions as everyone napped I quietly built a ramp up the front steps and down the back steps of the Quonset hut, then I opened both doors and ran my scooter between the beds lined up on each side as men showered me with shoes and bad language. For me it was fun.

Liquor could buy almost anything from the Seabees. I found my cot uncomfortable so I purchased a bed from them. They designed a wooden frame (of 2 x 4's) about 6'x4' set on legs to raise it about two feet. For springs they cut fighter plane innertubes (tires) into rubber bands and stretched them from side to side and lengthwise in a crossing pattern. It made for comfortable sleeping, at the expense of the government, and a fifth or two of liquor.

I also used liquor to purchase a stainless steel watch band and identification bracelet, adorned with cateye shells and fashioned out of Navy stainless steel serving trays.

On one sunny bright day when we were not scheduled for a bomb run, the silence of the day was broken by loud explosions coming from the airfield. We knew a mining mission had gone sour. We all counted one, then two until the count got to six, the number of mines being carried that day. The plane had cart wheeled on take off. The first explosion blew the tail section down the runway in the opposite direction of its flight. The tail gunner survived but the tail section did considerable damage to a parked plane, killing some ground personnel. The balance of the plane was totally destroyed as each mine exploded. The next day they buried ten wooden coffins. Rumor had it that they were empty boxes.

Letters to Lucille

Each day I mailed a letter to Lucille telling her of my daily activities and bombing missions. She matched them up with newspaper accounts of bombings and made them into a scrapbook. These letters formed the basis for much of the information included.

On Sunday morning, May 20th, her letter contained the vegetable seeds I had requested (from radishes to cantaloupes). All of the amateur gardeners decided to pitch in. With the soil being so rich and with the heat and rain, things grew quickly. However, washouts from the heavy thunderstorms were frequent, and devastating. Successful gardening became a challenge.

Two air fields had been built on Tinian. The 9th Bombardment Group flew from the North field which had four paralleling runways of 8,500 feet each, enabling four B-29s to take off at one time. It took six months for the Seabees to build the world's largest airfield after the island became secure in August 1944.

Training Continues

Part of our ongoing training was to learn how to parachute into the water. During the early flights from England to Germany many crewmen drowned after they were forced to bail out into the English Channel.

Unfortunately their chutes came down over them as they hit the water and they became tangled in the cords, making it impossible for them to swim. To correct this tragedy a new release mechanism was designed.

To participate in this training, we went down to the beach where a high tower had been constructed in the water. After putting on parachute harnesses without the chutes we simulated bailing out of a plane by jumping off the tower into the water using this newly designed release mechanism.

The new design made it possible for me to pull out a pin, hit a button on the parachute chest harness, allowing the chute to fly freely from me, then I made a free fall directly into the water. We practiced this technique over and over until it became routine. Our training continued as we practiced inflating our one man life rafts and the Mae West life preservers, named after the popular "figure eight" movie star.

After hitting the water we also trained to see how fast we could get in and out of a seven-man raft, the one carried inside the fuselage of the B-29 and used during a ditching operation. Each crewman also carried a one-man raft which he could use if he had to bail out. In addition to this training exercise we enjoyed a nice swim in the blue Pacific.

A few days later we were introduced to our squadron commander Lt. Colonel Malvern H. W. Brown. He informed us that he would join us on our first combat mission over Japan. He had a tough job. He stuck his neck out flying with each green crew making its first combat flight. Col. Brown also made preliminary training flights with us to practice for our combat missions. During these times we dropped live bombs on a nearby island, still occupied by stranded Japanese who were by-passed when the Marines took Tinian.

By now my bombing accuracy had greatly improved, which pleased Keller. I had scored a bull's eye several times. Our crew was even being considered for a lead position based on my accuracy.

When I first met my new pilot George Keller, I told him that my score was the highest average in my class. At first he thought he had the best bombardier. As he bragged about this he soon learned the truth and was furious, feeling that I had deceived him. I had not bothered to tell him that "highest" average was worst.

CHAPTER 7

Combat Begins

First Mission/May 18, 1945

My first combat mission took place on the night of May 18, 1945. Our instructions were to lay mines in the Bay of Tsuruca, Japan[8]. By the time we reached the target, the island was in complete darkness. I could not see my hand in front of my face, only the dials on the bomb sight that had been painted to glow in the dark. I could not visually see the target area, so we bombed by radar. Stan Levine, the radar operator did the sighting and informed me when to release the bombs. I dropped them by parachute into the harbor area while flying at an altitude of 5,000 feet. In order to get credit for completing this mission the Navy reviewed the exact location of the drop (coordinates) and the depth of the water before okaying it. The mines were set by the Navy to allow small ships to pass over safely; but would explode when a larger tonnage ship passed.

The mine manufacturers implanted a sensitive device in the mine, which could sense the amount of pressure on the water caused by a passing ship. The larger the ship's tonnage, the greater the pressure exerted on the mine as it laid on the floor of the ocean. The increased pressure caused it to explode. The importance of dropping them into the correct depth of water therefore became imperative.

---

[8]Ironically these are the same waters we found ourselves in after bail out. Source: war journal of 9th Bombardment Group.

At this time, Japanese shipping in the Pacific had come to a halt, but it continued from Japan to the Asian continent especially in the Sea of Japan via the Inland Sea and the Shimonoseki Straits. Our B-29s were able to mine these waters faster than the Japanese could clear the shipping lanes, causing havoc.

Participating in a mining operation required that each wing and center fuel tank be filled to its maximum. With the weight of seven mines each at 2,000 pounds, maximum fuel was required, without it, the mission could not have been accomplished. We also carried 200 rounds of ammunition for each gun.

B-29s were equipped with a portable toilet that could be removed from the plane after each flight. The standard operation procedure was, the crew member who used it first got to clean it. After cleaning the mess just one time, we all learned to hold off using it as long as possible. Everyone played the game, "who will be first?" As soon as used, the word spread quickly over the plane's intercom. If I had used it first they would say, "Let's all piss on Walter." The game took away the tension of the flight.

The presence of Col. Brown on our first mission relieved my fear. I did not envy his assignment. All of our training, to date, was about to be tested. I am not sure how I could have handled this without his assurance that all would go well.

Our first mission was successful. Everything went as planned. Thirty-six planes from our squadron participated without a casualty. Each plane flew the mission alone even over the target. On our own we were to pinpoint the correct coordinates (target area) and to be at the right altitude at release.

After each mission and following debriefing each crewman received a shot of whiskey from a medical corpsman. Since I did not drink, my navigator, Correll, stayed close by me to get my ration. I became his close buddy.

While on Tinian I was scheduled to participate in 17 bombing missions, between May 18th to August 8,

1945, including two mining missions, however, we were forced to abort once. On August 1, 1945, Air Force Day, the 38th birthday of the Air Force, eight hundred B-29s were scheduled to fly a bombing mission over Japan's mainland; their largest number to be airborne from any previous mission. We were scheduled to be one of the 47 B-29s from the 9th Bombardment Group. As we headed down the runway Keller did not like the way one of our engines was performing. He looked at his gauges and decided to pull off the runway and abort. A hord of Jeeps carrying colonels and generals ascended on him. Their first statement, "You better have a good reason for not taking off lieutenant." Once they examined the engines, they backed off. We were the only plane to abort.

As the result, I only received credit for completing 16 missions[9], and being awarded the airmedal with an oak leaf cluster.

On June 10, 1945, I wrote Lucille the following letter;

"This afternoon we had one of the best times since our arrival. Our uniform was shorts, shoes, cartridge belt, pistols and knives. To get to the water we Correll, Drew, Holden and I had to descend a cliff about 150 feet high. It is so steep you must use a rope to climb down. Down at the bottom are huge coral boulders. Close to the boulders and running into the water is a small sandy beach. Upon entering the water, the beach soon gives way to coral, very beautiful in color but tough on the feet. It slopes off gradually for about 50 yards, then there is a drop of about 30 feet. Here there are plenty of fish. We used goggles to see them. They were of all sizes up to a foot and all sorts of beautiful colors.

---

[9]See Appendix D page 167

After trying in vain to spear them, we tried catching them with a net, also without success. Just when you thought you had them, they would go into the cracks in the coral.

When we tired of swimming we laid on the beach for a while. Then we threw driftwood into the water and shot at it.

When we were out of ammo we climbed back up the cliff and returned to our Quonset."

Love,
Walter

During our 16 missions we were forced to land on Iwo Jima five times. Each time we were just plain out of gas. I thanked the Marines each time we landed for securing this island. They had paid a terrible price, and I appreciated it from a personal basis.

Iwo Jima

The United States armed forced turned the tide of World War II when it went on the offense in the South Pacific. By bringing together all the services, our country recaptured Japan, island by island. Each time we took another island, our goal became closer and closer.

Prior to using airfields in the Marianas, the B-29 flew out of Chakulia Indian; a long and dangerous flight over the hump to their forward base at Chengtu, located in China. It took six B-29s flying there to supply one B-29 to make a bombing run from Chengtu to Japan. Some of the supply planes used 12 gallons of fuel to deliver one gallon to Chengtu.

Eventually, we built air fields on Guam, Siapan and Tinian, in the Marianas. Finally, our B-29s were within striking distance of the main islands of Japan.

The invasion of Iwo Jima on February 19, 1945, by 75,000 Marines against 22,000 Japanese defenders ended when the Marines raised the American flag over Mt.

Surabachi under dangerous conditions[10]. The importance of moving onto Iwo Jima provided a safe haven for disabled B-29s returning from their bombing missions over Japan.

During the ground assault and Navy shelling, 19,000 Americans were wounded and 7,000 killed or died from wounds.

Iwo Jima, a black volcanic ash island situated between the Marianas and Japan is three miles wide and five miles long. On our first stop there it looked like a no man's land, without a tree, bush, or blade of grass. Most of the island had been destroyed by invading Marines, combined with the tremendous shelling by the naval guns off shore.

Thousands Saved

During my five precautionary landings on Iwo Jima I saw other disabled B-29s land under emergency conditions that otherwise would have crashed into the ocean.

In addition to giving B-29s a safe place to land, the newly acquired real estate gave a launching area for P-51 fighter planes. They protected B-29's while making their bomb runs. Because fighter planes had limited navigation abilities, the pilots returning from a flight over Japan, would form up with the B-29s and follow them back to Iwo Jima as they returned home to the Marianas. To the B-29 crews, the air support was invaluable in fighting off Japanese Zero fighter planes.

On one of our stops I saw as many as 100 B-29s making either emergency landings or fuel stops on Iwo Jima. I realized time and again what a price the Marines paid in lives to capture Iwo Jima; but in doing so they saved thousands of airmen's lives and B-29s. By the end of the war 2,400 B-29s made emergency landings on Iwo Jima involving 27,000 crewmen.

---

[10]This action of raising the flag was captured on film by photographer Joe Rosenthal and later created into a 100 ton sculpture by Felix deWeldon which stands in Arlington National Cemetery, Washington, DC.

During one of our overnight stays on the island we heard stories about surviving Japanese still living in caves and coming out at night to steal food and watch the movies. We were cautioned to be on alert at all times, and took their advice seriously.

Defying Aerodynamics

While waiting for our plane to be refueled during one of our stops, the most spectacular event I've have ever seen took place.

The pilot of a B-29 attempted to make a landing with two engines out on its left side. As the crippled plane approached the runway for its first landing, a smaller plane cut him off preventing him from landing. The pilot was forced to pull his crippled plane up and head for the open sea. Hundreds of servicemen lined the runway to watch.

My pilot and I were well aware of the instructions in the B-29 training manual stating that it is difficult for a plane with both engines out on one side to pull up and attempt another landing (almost impossible).

The pilot ordered, "Assume ditching positions."

Defying the manual he made a 360 degree turn while gaining altitude. His plane responded. The crowd increased, tension mounted as we watched this history-making event. He started another approach, lined his plane with the runway, and put his flaps and wheels down. It appeared he was going to attempt another landing. As the plane hit the runway his crew assumed they were in the ocean. Crew members, apparently assuming they had ditched the plane, jumped onto the wing and inflated the seven man raft contained in their fuselage. To their surprise, they were on dry land. They just stood there in amazement. At first I joined the others in laughing as to how comical this action appeared. Then our laughter turned to cheers and we stood, applauding the pilot at his spectacular landing.

Stop One

Our third bombing mission to Japan, June 1, 1945, ended by making our first fuel landing on Iwo Jima, saving us from ditching. We were simply out of gas.

During our approach to the target we encountered tremendous thermal clouds which had developed over the target area by the exploding bombs dropped ahead of us. We had previously read in Ripley's Believe It or Not a newspaper account by Sergeant T.L. Fenner of Brooklyn, New York, of the 483rd Bomb Squadron that during Fenner's mission over Tokyo the B-29s set off such a great explosion it blew a Japanese newspaper into their open bomb bay while flying at a height of 10,000 feet. At the time of reading, the event did not seem possible, until I saw the force of the thermal confronting us. As we turned to make our bomb run, the smoke appeared to be a huge thunderhead rising over Osaka to an altitude of 25,000 feet. Our squadron tried to go straight over the burning city as planned. The squadron leader found the conditions too dangerous. Forcing us to reassemble and take an alternate route around the rising thermals. Our action and that of others caused the burning area to become larger and larger as each wave of planes dropped their bombs. This regrouping used more gas than scheduled and required a refueling stop at Iwo Jima.

Stop Two

On the 7th of June we made our second bombing run on Osaka and for the second time ran low on fuel resulting in another stop at our favorite service station.

As we made our turn toward Osaka over the Sea of Japan, the target was clouded over, making us bomb by radar. By the time we reached the point where we released our bombs, the clouds were rising to a height of 30,000 feet. This additional climbing took a lot of fuel. On Iwo Jima we waited for over two hours before the fuel trucks got around to us.

Stop Three

"They're your bombs. Get rid of them."

George Keller, Airplane Commander

Our third precautionary landing developed on mission number seven when the navigator notified me that the bombs in the bottom rack in the forward bomb bay had not released and that the ones from the top rack had dropped and were bouncing on top of the lower ones. Bombs in a B-29 are installed on racks attached vertically from the ceiling of the plane to the catwalk. A wire from the rack runs through a hole in the arming pin in the nose of each bomb. At the end of this pin is a propeller that spins freely when the wire is pulled out as the bomb is released from the plane. As the propeller spins it screws the pin into the bomb, arming it to explode on contact. As our bombs released from their top position they pulled free of the wire and were bouncing around freely with the propellers in a position to spin and arm themselves. As the bombardier, it was my responsibility to release the bombs. The pilot ordered me to go back into the bomb bay and release them saying, "They're your bombs. Get rid of them."

The B-29 is constructed with a hatch door from the forward cabin into the bomb bay. A cat walk runs along either side of the bomb bay that is about six inches wide. To reach the bomb bay I had to open the hatch door which is about three feet in diameter with a one foot glass window for looking into the bomb bay to observe if all bombs had left the plane during each mission. With all of my equipment on it was a tight squeeze getting through the opening of the door. After passing through the opening, I had to take a giant step of about three feet over open space with nothing between me and the ground below. To reach the catwalk, it was indeed a "giant step." After establishing myself on it, I wedged myself between the bomb rack and the side of the plane to prevent me from falling, also freeing both hands so I could throw out the loose armed bombs. I knew the bombs bouncing around were volatile, my immediate concern was to get rid of them as soon as possible, one false move and the whole plane could blow up. I shoved, pushed, rolled and lifted each bomb free from those still held in place by the lower rack until one by one they disappeared into the darkness. I watched them explode as they hit the ground, hoping they were effective. Taking a screwdriver, I manually tripped the mechanism to release the lower rack of bombs, as they cleared the plane and fell, I breathed a sigh of relief. The crew applauded and cheered as I returned the way I left. For this action the pilot recommended me for a silver star, but his recommendation was rejected because, "It's the bombardier's responsibility to release the bombs. After all, they are 'his bombs.'

Stop Four

On our tenth mission over Wakayama, the number three engine caught fire over the target (maybe a hit by flak), forcing the pilot to put the plane into a steep dive in an effort to blow the fire out. The maneuver worked after we plunged several thousand terrifying feet in a matter of seconds. The thrust caused me to raise up out of my seat and hit the ceiling. This action consumed more gas than scheduled. After leveling off, the plane continued onto Tinian, via another refueling stop.

Stop Five

The standard operating procedure on a routine bombing run is to immediately close the bomb bay doors as soon as possible after the bombs leave the plane, any delay in closing increases a drag on the plane causing it to burn more fuel. However, on this particular mission over Uji-Yamada, July 28th, the bomb doors refused to close. I tried everything, I pushed, I pulled on my ejection lever. Finally in desperation I hollered to the pilot, "Use your emergency lever." It worked. Meanwhile, Japanese anti-aircraft locked their searchlights onto us. I can not remember a more frightening experience, feeling their lights locked in on us. The whole inside of the front cabin lit up so brightly I could read the time on my watch. Harmon, the gunner kept throwing metal tinsel, nicknamed "window," out of the plane. As it spread it appeared on the Japanese radarscreen like a large formation of planes, thus making it difficult for the anti-aircraft gun to identify or pick out any single plane. As a result, the search lights went haywire flashing here and there all over the sky, looking for us. The additional drag by the open bomb bay doors caused us to make another stop for more fuel on

Iwo Jima. I did not like these additional stops because I always feared hitting the ground, me first.
The Hole
Our sixth mission took us to the city of Yokkaichi. Our luck continued, this time we really were lucky. During our routine inspection of the plane on Tinian following our mission, one of the crewmen spotted a hole in the top of the fuselage above the bomb bays. After further investigation I saw that a Japanese shell had gone right through the open bomb bay and out the top of the plane, miraculously without exploding, escaping what could have been a major disaster, especially if it had gone through before our bombs had been released.

As always, I tried to hide the war from Lucille, on July 26, 1945, I wrote;
>Dear Lucille,
>Last night we had an enjoyable time, that is for over here.
>Gene Correll and I went to see the stage show "This is the Army." It was performed on the other side of the island, so our bomb group provided transportation. When we got there our seats were in the last row, so Gene went forward and found two empty seats. When we sat down Gene said, "Push over." I pushed a little, but the fellow next didn't move. Upon inspection, I found he was wearing a chicken and upon closer inspection discovered that the rest of the officers in the row were also colonels, here we were in the staff seats, but since we were there, we remained quiet, like we didn't know they were reserved seats. Naturally they were excellent seats, so we got a good view of the show.
>I believe the show was made up of the original cast that toured the States. You can well imagine how good it was. I

enjoyed it thoroughly. Since it was an all male cast, the female parts were a riot. Some, however, made up as beautiful girls. One of the biggest laughs was the strip-tease done supposedly by Gypsy Rose Lee.

Love,
Walter

The Nip Clipper

August 6th was a big day for the 9th Bombardment Group. Following our mission to the Maebashi Urban area (our 15th mission), we learned that the crew of the Nip Clipper, commanded by Maurice Ashland, had just completed 35 combat missions and was qualified to go home. Captain Jim Mulligan, group radar counter measures officer, also participated in the mission. Earlier that year, Col. Malvern Brown, a major at the time, handed the keys to this factory fresh shining clean B-29 to Lt. Maurice Ashland back at McCook Air Force base in Nebraska together with an invoice for $980,000 (the plane's cost).

The Ashland crew participated in the 9th Bombardment Group's first combat mission and flew all of their 35 missions in the Nip Clipper, hitting the designated target on every mission, without an air abort, never landing on Iwo Jima.

They were shot up some and crewmen Phenner and pilot Oleascheski, were hit by flak.

The potential most dangerous damage was unknown to them until landing after a night mission over the Shimoneseki Straights, then they could see that one half of the diameter of the blade near the hub had been shot away. If the blade had not held together, the engine would have been torn off, probably bringing the plane down.

During the later part of their missions their plane was selected for electronic counter measures under the direction of Capt. Mulligan. Holes were cut into its skin and antennas and black boxes were installed.

The Keller crew was excited about the Ashland crew going home because we were in line for inheriting the Nip Clipper.

CHAPTER 8

Last Mission/Yawata

The Assault

On Wednesday, August 8, 1945, the 20th Air Force made its all-out assault on Yawata, with an armada of 2,453 men in the air, aboard 233 Superfortresses (B-29). I participated in this raid with the Keller crew.

Three wings took part in the raid. Each wing consisted of three bomb groups made up of three squadrons. We were assigned to the number five position in the third squadron of the 9th Bombardment Group (313th wing). Each plane in the raid flew alone until it reached its rendezvous with the other planes in its squadron.

We usually flew the Sad Tomato, but it was not flight-ready for this mission. On our 15th mission over Maebashi we blew its #3 engine. As anticipated, we were assigned the Nip Clipper.

As standard operation procedure, prior to all combat missions, each crew member attended a briefing meeting; pilots to theirs, bombardiers to another and so on, followed by a combined group meeting. At the combined meeting, the commanding officer gives his best wishes for a safe return.

During these briefings the operational officer announced the target. We were informed that this would be a daylight mission using visual bombing since precision bombing would be required. Accuracy was essential. Only a daylight mission could provide this.

Our target was the city of Yawata, (known as the Pittsburgh of Japan because its principal industry; the production of steel) located on the northern end of the island of Kyushu just south of Honshu (the largest island in the Japanese Empire). Yawata had a population of 261,000 consisting of an area of 122 square miles.

Prior to the briefing we received our orders for the day as follows:

Briefing	2345
Mess (breakfast)	0030
Trucks to field	0145
To planes	0200

Pilot's Flimsy

At the briefing meeting each pilot received information contained in what became known as the pilot's flimsy, a secret document listing the airplane commander's name, the name of each crew involved in the mission, the plane's call letters, position in the bombing formation, the make up of the squadron, plane's number and time schedule as follows:

Marked Secret - Dated August 8, 1945

Time	Schedule
23:45	Briefing
00:30	Mess
01:45	Trucks
02:58	Start engines
03:05	Taxi
03:23	Take off

Smoke Signals	Route Alt.	Bombing Alt.
1st Air Sq -		
Red Smoke	5000-5800'	1st Sq - 19,000'
2nd Air Sq -		
Green Smoke	8000-8800'	2nd Sq - 19,800'
3rd Air Sq -		
White Smoke	11000-1180'	3rd Sq - 20,600'

Aldis Lamp Signals: Airspeeds[11]:
1st Air Sq - Red "W" Route   - 195
2nd Air Sq - Green "W" Assembly - 190
3rd Air Sq - White "W" Bombing - 195

Assembly
1st Air Sqdn. Assembles at 16,000' in left hand pattern. Depart Assembly at 1028

2nd Air Sqdn. Assembles at 17,000' in right hand pattern. Depart Assembly at 1029

3rd Air Sqdn. Assembles at 18,000' in left hand pattern. Depart Assembly at 1030

West Take-Off
1st Sq. Ships Start & Taxi 2 min earlier
99th Sq. Ships Start & Taxi 2 min later
5th Sq. Ships Start & Taxi at above times.

No Take Off After 0408. Any Take Off After 0358 CAS 200 Assembly

---

[11] This is indicated airspeed, the figure that shows on the airspeed indicator. Since this instrument operates on ram air pressure forced into a pilot tube as the aircraft moves forward, the indicated pressure drops with increase in altitude as the air grows less dense. This results in an increase in actual airspeed of about 2% per 1,000 feet of altitude. For pilot operational reasons, all air speeds are given an "indicated airspeed." Navigators, of course, would always use true airspeed then modify it in accordance with wind effect, to get groundspeed.

Flight Formation

1st Air Squadron

<u>Littlewood</u>*
    <u>Hendrickson</u>   <u>Linle</u>
  <u>Austin</u>   <u>Johnson</u>
<u>Vander Sheens</u> <u>Loy</u>   <u>Bundgard</u> <u>Donica</u>
    <u>Feil</u>   <u>Schlosherg</u>

2nd Air Squadron

<u>Rogan</u>*
  <u>Prehoda</u> <u>Bertagnoli</u>
  <u>Payne</u>   <u>McMahan</u>
<u>Petersen</u> <u>Lassman</u>   <u>Eichler</u> <u>Dennell</u>

3rd Air Squadron

<u>Nash</u>*
<u>Barned</u> <u>Garbor</u>
  <u>Reynolds</u>   <u>Tulloch</u>
<u>Miller</u> <u>Carpi</u>   <u>Nelson</u> <u>Keller</u>
                <u>Barneyback</u>

*Lead Crew Stripe   Marked Secret

Also, we received instructions about additional personnel who would be on the mission, i.e. staff members or observers, etc.

Our crew was assigned the call letters circle X 23. For visual identification the number 23 was painted on both sides of the fuselage. A large circle was painted on both sides of the plane's vertical stabilizer with an X inside to identify the plane as part of the 9th Bombardment Group.

As we entered the mess hall, Keller met two of his new found buddies, Scotty Tulloch and Gordon Nelson, both aircraft commanders and seasoned flyers. They were scheduled to fly in our formation. Nelson was married and came from the San Antonio area. He had flown B-17s prior to flying B-29s. Tulloch was born in Morenci, Arizona, in 1915. He and Betty were married in 1944, just before his going overseas. Before coming to Tinian he flew B-17s and B-24s as an instructor pilot. Keller said, "I'll meet you at the assembly area."

We ate a hearty breakfast of juice, oatmeal, pancakes with fried eggs on top, butter, syrup and coffee, then piled into a truck for a bumpy ride to the airfield to conduct our pre-flight inspection of the plane. As we approached the Nip Clipper, we noticed that the ground crew was removing the final parts of the radar countermeasures equipment from the plane.

Then we met Lt. Ervin Czyzewski walking toward Capt. Hal Lassman's plane. I asked Ervin, "What is going on?" He replied, "Since Ashland's crew is not flying the Nip Clipper any more, Capt. Mulligan gave orders to remove the extra RCM gear, antenna receivers, analyzers and added transmitter and move it to Lassman's plane." He continued, "The reason Mulligan gave was that he did not know who would be flying Ashland's plane, and he wanted to be sure it went to an experienced crew, so he moved it." Lt. Czyzewski said, "On this Yawata mission, since it is my turn to fly with the RCM equipment, I will not be flying in the Nip Clipper. I'll be flying with the Lassman crew, with my back to the radar operator using the aromatic 'honey bucket' for my seat." He said, "Good bye and good luck with the Nip Clipper."

Each crew member, using his published checklist, made a thorough inspection at his position to make sure everything listed functioned correctly. Then while the pilot sat at his position in the plane, the crew lined up in front of each engine and, one by one, each man put his shoulder to each propeller blade and, while pushing, turned the engine as the next fellow in line did the same thing to the next blade as it came around. Each engine was pulled through 14 blades to insure that no oil had leaked into the lower cylinder of the radial engine, starting an engine with an oil block could ruin it. After all the engines had turned over, the pilot started the engine. This procedure took place with each engine until all were running. Upon completion the pilot waited until he received orders from the tower to proceed to the runway.

Take Off

We paused at the beginning of the runway awaiting the signal from the tower to take off, both pilots pressed their feet to their brake pedal as hard as possible as Keller revved up the four engines to their maximum. The plane shook and quivered as it remained in place. Since we were loaded to capacity with maximum bombs and fuel, it was imperative to get as fast a start as possible to get airborne.

As we waited for the signal to start down the runway I could see runway activity before me as if I was in a movie. Sitting in the greenhouse provided me with a good vantage point to observe the actions unfolding. I watched as each plane ahead of us gathered more and more speed, then disappeared at the end of the runway as it dropped below the runway's level.

Tinian rose from 50 to 100 feet above the ocean, creating a cliff at the end of our runway. As each plane left the ground and cleared the edge of the cliff it settled down below the level of the runway, hopefully, skimming just above the water as it accelerated. I kept my fingers crossed as I watched each plane disappear and prayed a little that he would make it. "I see him. I see him!" I shouted to the pilots as the plane came into my sight as it gained altitude.

Our time to take off was fast approaching. My heart began to pound. Then at 0313 on orders from the tower, Keller and Holden released the pressure on the brakes and the plane literally lunged forward as we sped down the runway.

During takeoff, I had to sit up front in the Greenhouse. As our plane settled down below the level of the cliff and skimmed just above the white caps I felt as if I could drag my feet into the water. Finally, we started to ascend. Take off was always scary for me. It seemed to take forever before we began to climb.

After reaching flying altitude our plane flew alone until we reached the assembly area. In the meantime, the navigator calculated the plane's heading and relayed the information to the pilot. When it got light, I used the crosshair in the Norden bomb sight to calculate the plane's drift. I did this just like over land, except I selected a white cap on the water and adjusted the hair in the bomb sight to keep it on track. The white cap appeared to be running down the hair from the 12 o'clock to the 6 o'clock position. This procedure allowed me to establish the amount of the plane's drift. The navigator did the same thing with his driftmeter and we verified each other's calculations. The new heading was relayed to the pilot and the plane's direction was corrected to reflect the amount of drift. Technically, this "dead reckoning" procedure means calculating position by recording time and track over the ground (in this case, water). Drift was one of the factors entering into track. Dead reckoning, therefore, means without aid of external navigational aids or celestial navigation.

During the night the navigator used a sexton to determine our position by determining the location of the stars and our relation to them. He sighted out the dome window on the top of the plane to plot our position, then gave the pilot a new heading.

For security reasons there were no radio signals available to assist us in navigating the plane. We had to rely on dead reckoning and/or the sexton.

The purpose of this mission was to eliminate Yawata's capability to produce steel. A successful bombing mission could shorten the war.

We left Tinian at 0313 carrying a bomb load of 24 m-17 amiable clusters of 500 pounds each for a total of 6.3 tons of incendiary bombs. We headed for the assembly area to be reached in seven hours at 1030.

Our four R-3350 Wright Double Cyclone radical engines each swinging four blade propellers of 16 feet in diameter, pulled us closer and closer toward our target.

My interim duties were to verify the plane's drift and report my readings to the navigator. I also acted as an observer for the pilot watching for other planes, both friendly and hostile. It became difficult not to doze off between my readings with the constant hum drum of the engines. My position in the nose of the plane put me just in front of both pilots and at about the level of their feet making it easy for them to kick me in the head with their boots when they saw my head drop down whenever I dozed off.

The plane was well balanced, after the aircraft commander completed trimming the plane, i.e. adjusting the flaps, air speed, etc. to get it into a perfect alignment for conserving fuel consumption. If I moved to the back of the plane, the shift of my weight could cause the plane to lose speed and consume more fuel. I became a prisoner to my seat. Keller would not let me wander around in the plane, without cause.

News of the Atomic Bomb

Just as the pilot notified the crew that we were approaching the target area and to be on the lookout for enemy planes, our radio operator Martin Zapf picked up word that the Americans had dropped a new type of bomb. Although the information was sketchy we learned that this bomb was carried by a B-29 and had totally destroyed a Japanese city.

Zapf's report confirmed rumors we had heard before take off. We had no knowledge of it, except rumors. Several days earlier I wrote the following to my wife:

> "There are all sorts of speculations today on the possibilities of a new type of bomb. Everyone is hoping that Japan will give up after seeing its destructive power. Let's hope so."

Enola Gay Story

Just two days before I left on our 16th mission, the B-29 plane we had just heard about (with its 11 man crew) dropped the first atomic bomb to be used in combat on the city of Hiroshima, located on the island of Honshu. Airplane commander Paul Tibbets[12] named the Enola Gay after his mother.

Prior to Enola Gay's mission to Hiroshima, I remember that a new outfit arrived on Tinian which had a certain mystique about it, something special. They never associated with the other crews on the island. Their barracks were encircled with a double barb wire fence, with a guard marching between the fence 24 hours a day. No one was allowed to contact them. There was a degree of jealously among us about their privileges.

The crew of the Enola Gay left the island of Tinian in the Marianas at 0245 with the atomic bomb, nicknamed Little Boy, and dropped it on Hiroshima at 0815 from an altitude of 31,000 feet on August 6, 1945, (August 5th in Washington, D.C.), totally destroying the

---

[12]Paul Tibbets the pilot of the Enola Gay carried the first atomic bomb that was dropped on Hiroshima he was asked by a little girl while he was giving a speech "What were your feelings toward dropping the atomic bomb and how do you deal with your grief regarding the people who died?" He answered, "Dropping the bomb. I look at that as a military wartime assignment as the use of any available weapon to bring about the defeat of an enemy of the U.S." He believed it would bring an end to the fighting and save more lives on both sides.

Regarding his grief he states, "I took an impersonal position and refused to accept responsibility for any act of war." He concluded that it is hard for young people to understand the potential consequences that the attack on Pearl Harbor opened up to this country and its people.

city. This bomb was equivalent to between 8,000 and 15,000 tons of TNT. Previously 2,000 B-29s had been needed to carry that much explosive power using conventional bombs[13] (as in the Tokyo raid of March 4, 1945).

Following the dropping of the atomic bomb, the Japanese military forces built a massive defense of Hiroshima and throughout Japan. A Japanese officer prepared his men by justifying their withdrawal from the Marianas in favor of a strong defense on their home islands. Japan had not lost a war since 1598 and they would deal with the Americans and allies by assembling a vast army to prevent an invasion[14]. St. Francis Xavier (cira 1549) expressed that Japan (Nippon, Land of the Rising Sun) was very concerned about honor. Honor above all. Under strict discipline, each Japanese officer drove his men to combat readiness. The city of Hiroshima controlled a communications system linked to the armed fortresses being built throughout the island of Honshu. To inflict maximum casualties on the invaders, more than 45,000 troops assembled in Hiroshima in addition to the small Kamikaze boats located in the harbor manned by Japanese sailors willing to sacrifice their lives for the Emperor by ramming their boats into the invader's boats. The commanders of Hiroshima informed their troops (and wanted the Emperor to believe) that future atomic bombs could not touch them if they went underground (based on the fact that the first bomb exploded above ground).

Following the Allies' victory in Europe, diplomats met in Potsdam July 26, 1945, and issued an ultimatum to Japan followed by dropping leaflets[15] on the cities

---

[13]The United States could now use one plane armed with one bomb to do as much destruction as exposing 22,000 airmen in 2,000 planes. The only difference was that 130,000 Japanese casualties resulted from just one bomb. Dead is dead, however.

[14]See Appendix E page 168.

[15]Marching to work at Niigat on 27 July 1945 Shillito (a P.O.W. from New Mexico National Guard) saw thousands of leaflets falling around them. The guards were going crazy trying to keep them from picking the leaflets up.

warning the civilians of pending bombing of great magnitude[16].

Japan had given up her spoils, island by island, but grimly continued to fight while bombers bombed city after city, raining terror over Japan.

The estimated death toll of Japanese by July, 1945, totalled more than three million persons in the field and on the Japanese homeland, including as many as 800,000 civilians.

On July 8, 1945, a month before the atomic bomb was dropped, a pilot by the name of Aufford from the 9th bomb group dropped twelve 500 pound propaganda leaflet bombs on the cities of Nobeoka, Usuki and Kochi. On July 11, 1945, he dropped the same amount of leaflets on Masuda, Tsuwano, Kuga and Kawanoishi warning the citizens of future increased bombings.

War Minister Korechika answered the Potsdam Declaration stating that in the past not a single enemy soldier had ever set foot on Japan's sacred soil and they expected to continue to repulse any invading force with heavy losses to them. The ultimatum was of no great value to Japan and they would continue fighting. When the Japanese failed to respond to the Potsdam Declaration, President Truman made his decision to use the atomic bomb, weather permitting, as soon as possible following August 3, 1945. Some advised it would not end the war[17] but would jeopardize all prisoners of war in Japan.

Tony King (P.O.W.) deciphered one. They were copies of Potsdam Declaration. Japan could surrender unconditionally or be destroyed. The weapon of that destruction though not named, would be the atomic devise recently - some later said fittingly - perfected high on a New Mexico plateau and successfully tested in a New Mexico desert.

The leaflet deciphered by King contained another warning: Evacuate the town immediately, it counseled. The P.O.W. uneasily wondered why. (Source, Beyond Courage by Dorothy Cave) (Additional source confirmed by Lt. Fukui.)

[16] Source: Walter Hunt, USAF retired.

[17] "There has been breast beating by some over the use of the atomic bomb but all the P.O.W. I talked with were convinced the atomic bomb had saved their lives."

On August 4, 1945, B-29s based on Tinian showered thousands of leaflets on those cities[18] who were potential targets for the atomic bomb. The leaflets stated "evacuate your civilians." Most inhabitants ignored the warning[19].

The allies replied to Korechika's answer with the atomic bombing of Hiroshima on August 6, 1945, while continuing with its normal bombing operations. One of those bombing raids was the very raid I write of.

Japan, August 8, 1945

As we neared Yawata, we were unaware of the destruction, panic, anger and frustration harbored by the inhabitants.

The Japanese civilians had survived the massive fire bombing of Tokyo on March 9 and 10, 1945, during which time the city of six million witnessed the largest night raid by B-29s on one of their cities.

This first low level night incendiary raid ordered by General Curtis LeMay designated urban Tokyo as its target. The city was important to the Japanese war effort as an important communication and railroad center, manufacturing 95 percent of all radio equipment, 75 percent of all telephone equipment, 90 percent of all aircraft cannon. 30 percent aircraft engines, 10 percent all aircraft. 6 percent auto and motors. 30 percent ball bearings and 37 percent refinings.

"The Japanese told them I would be executed if American forces invaded their homeland.

"All indications were that the Japanese were being schooled to defend every square foot of their soil with their lives. P.O.W.'s told me of seeing factories where bamboo spears were being made as weapons for women.

"If the atomic bombs had not been dropped then the fleet would have moved in. A multitude of sunken ships and beaches littered with an army of dead would have resulted. We and the enemy might have counted our dead in millions. The atomic bomb spared us that tragedy."
     Mark Clutter, Writer VFW Magazine
     September 1985

[18]U.S. Intelligence reports indicated there were no P.O.W.'s being held captive in these cities.
[19]Confirmed by Fukui.

According to group commander Col. Henry Hughlin's log entry, the 9th Bombardment Group had 32 aircraft airborne participating in this raid over Tokyo. One made an early return, three did not find target, two crews ditched. The crews witnessed searchlights during their bombing runs. Average bombing load per plane was 13,100 pounds. Average gross weight of plane was 134,800. Average fuel consumption was 5,696 gallons. Following the successful mission, commendations were made by Gen. Hap Arnold for LeMay to the 6th, 9th, 504th and 505th groups.

On August 6, 1945, the Japanese became victims of another type of bomb which they could not understand or comprehend, the atomic bomb.

Attack on Yawata

After a seven hour flight from Tinian we reached our assembly area, or rallying point, a predetermined invisible spot in the sky identified by coordinates, located by the navigator from his calculations. He directs the pilot to it. For this mission the assembly area was located at 18,000 feet. (The coordinates were known only by the navigator.) At about 1030 I saw two planes scheduled to make up our formation. "There they are!" I shouted. Scotty Tulloch was assigned the lead position. We took our position on his right wing and Gordon Nelson on his left to form a wedge. Our three planes joined six others to make up our air squadron and a larger wedge. Two other air squadrons joined us to make the 9th Bombardment Group. Our wedge consisted of 30 planes. We joined two other groups to form the 313th wing. Three wings under the 20th Air Force formed into a striking force and proceeded toward the target. The armada, acting together, consisted of 223 planes, with a striking force of 1,400 tons of bombs. The weather was excellent, a bright clear morning, making it possible to see the target clearly. During our briefing on Tinian, Gene Correll, our navigator, had been given the coordinates of the target. I had received a map pinpointing where to drop my bombs.

As our plane approached the target, we observed a plane ahead of us in another formation going down in flames. We watched the parachutes unfold as we all expressed our sorrow and dismay knowing how prisoners were treated, especially airmen. It became a sight I will never forget.

Prior to dropping our bombs, the pilot was having difficulty holding his place in the formation. We were lagging behind the other planes. This made us vulnerable to fighters. Keller could not hold his position for reasons not known to me. I could hear Holden yelling, "Pull up into formation, we're falling back!" I was too busy preparing for my bomb run, but I heard Keller holler back, "I can't. I'm losing power!" By that time everyone in the front compartment was getting into the act, knowing a lone plane out of formation was vulnerable. In spite of our lagging, our bomb run was progressing as planned. The bomb bays were opened and I released our bombs at about 1120. To add to our plight, four bombs failed to release. They were hung-up on the bomb rack in the bomb bay. Correll, the navigator who was closest to the window in the bomb bay entry door, saw them and yelled the information to me. That's all we needed, but we did have some luck. During this run over the target when Zeros targeted in on us, our P-51 fighter planes from Iwo Jima started dogfighting with them, at our three o'clock position, but as the Zeros were driven off flak began bursting all around us. We were engaged in combat against the enemy. I am not sure if any of our gunners got any shots off, probably not, for fear of hitting one of the bombers or fighters. During all of this confusion, I was desperately pulling on my bomb salvo release level without success. Finally, I yelled to the pilot, "Release your salvo lever." It worked. The bombs dropped.

CHAPTER 9

Nip Clipper Takes Hit

Bail Out

Flak continued to burst all around us. Just as the last bomb dropped, the right gunner, Sergeant Traverse Harman, yelled over the intercom, "The right wing is on fire, we have been hit." I could not tell if the hit was either by flak or fighter planes. "The gas tank in the right wing had ignited," Harmon yelled. "Flames are trailing back as far as the tail section. The fire is intensifying," he screamed. From his position, the pilot could operate two fire extinguishers mounted in the engine. It had worked before, but this time the CO_2 failed because our fuel tank rather than the engine was on fire. I felt the plane could explode at any time. We were on a northerly course which would take us directly over the island of Honshu. To avoid it, the pilot turned to the left (west), away from Japan toward the Sea of Japan in the direction of Okinawa. The thought of ditching or bailing out had never occurred to me. We had never practiced this situation during training, only in theory. Still in flames, the pilot put the plane in a dive at 400 mph in an attempt to fan out the fire. Our descent took us from 20,600 feet to 5,000 feet in a matter of minutes. Instead of putting the fire out, the flames intensified, and he decided to ditch. Keller bellowed, "Assume ditching positions."

Under normal conditions, we would land the plane into the water, with wheels up and skim the plane on its belly to a stop. The plane should remain afloat long enough for the crew to jettison the large life raft contained in the fuselage, jump into it and leave the area before the plane either blew up or sunk.

During standard ditching operation, each crew member removes his chute and life raft, assumes a sitting position facing rear with his back supported against a sturdy (upright) panel in the plane. He braces his head and knees to reduce the chances of injury.

When Keller commanded "Assume position," the crew began scurrying around in the forward compartment; putting on equipment, taking some off, getting a last gulp of water, trying to locate their ditching positions. It was a mad house. (I am sure the same was happening in the rear compartment.)

Keller continued the plane in a dive. Meanwhile, I could not close the bomb bay doors from my position, my closing mechanism had been damaged when we took the hit, now it would be suicide to ditch with open bomb bays. The plane would bust wide open on impact and explode. The situation got very hectic.

After my failure to close the doors from my position I jumped up and quickly moved through the forward compartment toward the entrance of the bomb bay.

I turned the handle on the hatch door leading into the bomb bay, which I had done before, so I knew what to expect. After I opened the door, I stopped momentarily, took a deep breath looked out over a massive area of emptiness before me, all the way down to the ocean and proceeded. I had a difficult time making it through the door. It was a tight squeeze with my life raft, Mae West jacket, as well as my parachute, all of which made for a bulky situation.

I took a giant step from the door to the catwalk. One slip and I would be out of the plane. After reaching the catwalk I laid down on my belly while holding onto the bomb rack with one hand. With the other I reached out and grabbed the handle provided for closing the bomb bay doors during emergencies like this. I shifted my position to get a better grip on the handle. I stretched out as far as possible. It seemed like forever as I watched the water getting closer and closer. The doors would not budge. It seemed hopeless. Realizing my efforts were futile, I decided to return to the forward compartment. By this time the ocean was getting ever closer. I stood up and made that giant step back toward the hatch door, and stepped inside.

As I reentered the front cabin I found it empty except for Keller, who was trying to hold the plane steady at about 3,000' so everyone could bail out safely. He turned and yelled to me, "Bail out[20], jump! Jump!" He had already let the wheels down emptying the nose wheel well as an exit for the men in the forward compartment. The hatch cover had been left opened by them when they bailed out. While I stood straddled over the opening, I looked out the right window and saw the flames trailing from the wing. I could stay and die or risk my life by jumping. I wrapped my hand around the rip cord, rolled over and went out. I must have closed my eyes because the next thing I knew I was gliding toward the sea.

A hero to the end, Keller stayed with the plane until everyone got out safely. He even waited for me as I worked in the bomb bay. I am not sure I would or could have jumped without Keller commanding me to jump. I owe my life to him.

Hitting the Water

As the final member to leave the plane before George Keller, I was the last person to see him alive. Gliding down, I looked up just as I hit the water and saw him coming down with his chute partially open. He hit the water about the same time as the plane hit and exploded. Burning debris littered the ocean area where Keller entered the water. No one saw him again.

After stabilizing myself in the ocean I pulled the string on the Mae West and inflated it, then the life raft, and climbed inside (both had a bottle of compressed air built into them for inflating purposes).

---

[20]See Appendix F page 169

Behind me I heard tailgunner Christus Nikitas yelling for help. He could not swim. He did not have a Mae West vest or life raft on. They had been removed in preparation for ditching. He had to crawl from the tail position to the rear bomb bay to bail out. He coughed, flailed his arms, and gasped for air, all the time, yelling again and again for help.

"Nick, I'm coming," I yelled to him. I removed my shoes in order to make it easier to swim, but with the life raft bobbing up and down, untying the wet laces seemed to take forever. I jumped in, kept my head above water so I would not lose him (like I had learned in the Boy Scouts). I dragged my one man life raft behind me and swam toward him, then hauled him onto my life raft and towed him to the others.

Once I'd secured him inside the raft, I saw the crew was strung out over a considerable distance, the size of a football field. Everyone hollered, waved, doing everything possible to get each other's attention. It's amazing to me that we all got together, being spread out over such a large area.

As I towed Nikitas towards the others, I began counting heads as we swam toward an imaginary spot in the water. The sea was relatively calm (a break for us). One by one, I saw them coming closer, waving, shouting. Five, six, then seven. Finally eight. Except for Keller we were all accounted for. Survivors of the bailout. Finally together, we caught our breath, thankful that we were still alive. And then, I took inventory of our supplies. It did not look too good.

Those who did not have life jackets were helped into our four rafts. Exhausted, the others hung on while treading water.

With all our flailing about, I feared we had attracted sharks. With six of us hanging in the water, we were easy meat. I wanted the submarines. They are supposed to be here. How would we manage? "Where are they?" I shouted angrily.

We were ten survivors in the water, west of the island of Honshu, Japan, with just four one-man life rafts, some water, and three C-1 vests containing candy charms, chocolate, bullion cubes, fishing gear, paddles and a sail. We were in trouble.

In the confusing shift from ditching orders to bail out, only four of us managed to leap with one man life rafts. These would have to support ten men. "How could we handle this?" I asked.

On past missions, we had never used our C-1 vest. They were bulky along with all our other gear we wore. Our attitude was, "Why wear them? We will never need them." Except for the three who wore them, the rest made a bad call. This time they were wrong, which could cost us our lives. The three men with the vest had a tough decision to make. Should they share their rations with the others? This could have been a sticky situation for me. Both pilots had been in command while the plane was in the air, but now that command fell on me since we were no longer flying. I out-ranked Holden.

I was relieved that I did not have to make a command decision. All three men turned over their rations to me for general distribution. Fortunately, they shared without question. Our first crisis passed without discussion. Sharing would be our means of survival.

Each vest contained supplies sufficient to sustain one man for only a few days. To stretch the supplies from three vests to sustain ten men would require rationing under strict discipline.

We were in an untenable situation until two planes from our formation appeared, hovered, and began dropping supplies. One plane <u>Patches Crosstown 33</u> was piloted by aircraft commander Scotty Tulloch, the other by Lt. Gordon Nelson. Their accuracy was not too good, since they had never done this before, so supplies were scattered all over the ocean. Those who could swim left the sanctuary of the rafts and swam out to retrieve them before they sank. It became a real scramble, "There's one," someone would holler, "There's another." Much of the equipment sank upon impact with the water[21], but we did manage to salvage four additional life rafts and a radio transmitter named Gibson Girl after its shape of a small waist. The transmitter was a yellow cube about one foot wide. The hand cranking mechanism for generating power looked like bicycle pedals.

After Tulloch and Nelson dropped their supplies our new inventory consisted of:
- (8) eight one-man rafts
- (3) three C-1 vests
- (4) four canteens of water
- (5) five cans of water (about a pint each, that came with the life rafts)
- (1) flare pistol with flares.

The two pilots stayed overhead as long as possible but as their fuel ran low, they had to leave us and head for Okinawa.

As they left our area and slowly disappeared, the last contact with our friendly world faded away, and we began drifting.

Day One (Wednesday)[22]

By early afternoon we had successfully brought all eight rafts together. We tied them into one big raft using belts, shoelaces and anything else we could find. The rafts had canvas handles on the outside which made it easier for securing them.

We soon learned that a life raft is not the most comfortable place to sit. The inside dimensions are such that a man's hip fits snugly into the back end and with legs extended, his feet touch the forward inside portion of the raft. The blue bottom starts about six inches below

---

[21] Scotty Tulloch and Gordy Nelson's actions were instrumental in making it possible for the Keller crew to survive their stay in the Sea of Japan for seven days. Both airplane Commanders had been assigned to the 9th Bomb Group since its days at McCook Air base in Nebraska. As a replacement crew, the Keller crew, met Tulloch and Nelson when assigned to their squadron on Tinian and flew together in the same flight formation with them on this mission.

[22] Source: Co-pilot Carl Holden and I independently kept diaries while in P.O.W. camp, capturing the daily events as they took place.

the bright yellow sides. The entire raft is made of heavy rubberized material, with an outside measurement of about six feet by three feet.

At best, even for a little fellow the quarters were cramped. Each raft rode high in the water until a second man was added, then it sank deeper to within about two inches above the water. The bottom is very flexible so that you could feel the movement of the water patting your rear end.

Ten men and eight rafts meant we had to make some quick decisions. We could let two men stay in the water at all times, and change positions frequently, which would mean that everyone would be wet all of the time. Under this scenario, we were in constant danger of capsizing each time a man in the water got back into the raft. And then, there was the threat of sharks. Our second option was to have two men ride on top of two other men. This seemed to be the best of a bad situation even though water splashed inside constantly. Waves splashed continuously over the sides. Each time we shifted crewmen from one raft to another, we took on more water. The weight of the top man pressing on the man underneath, made this arrangement difficult for both men. We changed positions frequently from raft to raft and from the top position to the bottom. Repositioning became a delicate maneuver; we had to be very careful not to capsize. Our hopes were high that the Air Sea Rescue team with their submarine would be coming soon.

During all combat missions from Tinian to Japan there was a network of Air Sea Rescue teams made up of a submarine and a B-29, working as a team. The B-29s, known as Super Dumbo's named after the heroic flying elephant of Walt Disney movies, flew in a small circle over a submerged submarine, maneuvering at a designated coordinate in the sea. These teams were spaced at intervals along the route taken by the bombers going to and from the target. A radio code system was designed whereby a disabled plane could contact the Dumbos and submarines for help. They in turn would get the coordinates of the disabled plane and go to its aid. Some Dumbos were outfitted with droppable life boats and other rescue equipment. This was a very successful operation. It was upon this air/sea rescue team that we pinned our hope on for an immediate rescue.

We were a well-disciplined crew as a result of the invaluable training we received on Tinian. Our practicing sessions with the life rafts and simulating bail outs, helped considerably.

Radio operator Marty Zapf held the Gibson girl in between his legs and cranked the handles with fervor, while we all anxiously looked on knowing this machine could be our contact with the outside world, especially the Dumbos. We blocked out all nuisance waves, wanting desperately to make the radio work. As a radio operator, he had not been trained to repair the equipment. He cranked and cranked, hitting the radio again and again but we heard only silence. Just silence. It was a useless item and only increased our weight. Therefore, it had to be ditched with regrets and full honors.

We continued wondering how the rescue units would find us? I was certain Tulloch and Nelson had contacted the Air Sea Rescue team, but did Keller have time to make radio contact prior to bail out? The only answers came with a slow breeze and salt spray on my badly chapped lips.

I said to the group, "I'm not sure I could have bailed out without Keller's help."

Holden was understandably irritated. "We should not have been in this situation in the first place. He should have kept up with the formation."

After settling into the rafts and positioning the one man on top of another man, we told our personal versions of our bailouts, as if replaying it would diminish our helplessness. Our stories were the same, each using different quirks. The composite picture was when orders were changed from ditching to bail out all of the crewmen obviously were able to get their chutes on, but only three others beside me had sufficient time to grab their one man life rafts and reattach them to their parachute harness before bailing out. I had attached mine before going into the bomb bay.

I replied how surprised I was to re-enter the plane and find everyone had bailed out except Keller. "Suppose I had not come back in time," I said. "I would have gone down with the plane without knowing about the change in orders."

Someone said, "As I neared the water I hit the button on the parachute harness on my chest to release the chute, for a free fall feet first into the water just like we had practiced."

We all agreed, "the trick was to release the chute at the optimum time, not too high up, not too close to the water for a safe entry." I had practiced this technique on Tinian, always thinking it might be important for someone else to know. Because of our training, our actions became some what routine.

Carl Holden, who was over six feet tall, said, "During bail out as I left the plane through the nose wheel well opening, I hit my head so hard on the side of the wall, I was knocked unconscious. When I regained consciousness I found myself floating towards the water."

Gene Correll, the navigator, explained, "I wrapped my fingers around the chain on my canteen of water and successfully hung on to it." The crew members welcomed the extra water.

I could not fault Holden's expressions that Keller tried to conserve gas by lagging behind the formation but I was quick to state, "Keller held the plane steady and on course until everyone got out safely. He jeopardized his own life by staying with the plane until the last minute. Keller did remain calm during an adverse situation." I thought to myself, "I might not have made it had he not."

Radar Navigator Stan Levine said, "Just as I hit the water I had the crap scared out of me. What to do? How could I get my flight suit off? Bad enough getting out of the one piece suit when not in the water. After my successful bowel movement I struggled again getting it back on." Everyone laughed. It was a big joke to all of us and broke the tension.

We soon began talking about the good food we would be getting when the American submarine arrived. "Especially the steaks," Nick answered.

I said, "If the Army had honored its commitment when I enlisted in the camouflage unit, I would not be in this predicament."

Someone confidently replied, "But you wouldn't have this experience to talk about when you get home."

During the ensuing hours the hot sun shone brightly on us. We did not have any protection against the sun's rays. The water stayed relatively calm. As the sun set, for the first time we realized our chances of rescue at night were slim[23].

About midnight of the first night, a Japanese boat of some kind came pump, pump, pumping nearer and nearer toward us from out of the darkness. Navigator Correll explained to us that the moon was in its "new moon phase" and it would be very dark tonight reducing visibility. Our fears mounted as it came closer and closer. It came so close we could hear the voices of the sailors talking on board. We hunched down as low as possible to reduce our profile and remained absolutely quiet. As we huddled, our thoughts turned to, yes, we could yell out and be rescued from the sea, but as prisoners of war. No way. Waiting for our submarines seemed a better alternative. The ship made a black image against the dark sky line as it passed without incident to within 25 feet of us. We supposed it was looking for us. Afterwards, we pointed out the various constellations and planets which helped take our minds away from our plight.

Day Two (Thursday)

At sunrise on August 9, 1945, the beginning of our second day at sea we could no longer see the small

---

[23]By the end of our first day the 9th Bombardment Group issued a secret consolidated mission report #313, dated 8/8/45, Yawata urban area. See Appendix G page 171.

island that was visible the first day. During the night, we had drifted in a northeasterly direction.

The warmth of the rising sun on our faces felt good. It warmed my body from the cool of the night and gave me comfort. It had been a very dark night. The only ray of light came from the blinking stars. I was frightened all night. It was so very dark and wet. I never knew it could be so dark. As a city boy I had always seen light reflecting from the city. The only noise we could hear after the boat passed was the splashing of the water licking the sides of the rafts. The sun was a real comfort as it began to dry the top part of my flight suit. The sea was relatively calm with swells which caused our rafts to go up and down.

Our drifting continued to the northeast. We began our routine rotation of men from top to bottom, and raft to raft.

In the early morning we saw U.S. planes off in the distance flying in what looked like a search pattern, hopefully looking for us. We dumped sea marker dye into the water and flashed our mirrors, all of which had been included in the equipment found in the life rafts. Also included were flares which we fired into the air in an effort to attract their attention. One flare malfunctioned and fell back into the raft. We scrambled, frantically trying to douse the flare. At a great risk of getting burned, we all tried using our bare hands to scoop it up. Someone was successful and tossed it overboard. We could have lost a raft which would have been a disaster. One by one, I could feel the men panic. It took a long time for everyone to calm down after we successfully got rid of it.

The planes continued flying on the horizon at an estimated altitude of about 7,000 to 8,000 feet. Unfortunately they did not pick up our distress signals, leaving us disappointed, and in dispair. As we drifted west of the Japanese island of Honshu, we really did not know our location. Navigator Correll explained, "We must be entering the Shimonoseki Straits and into the Sea of Japan from my final calculations before bail out."

Walter R. Ross shown after receiving his bombardier wings..
Photo taken at Albuquerque, New Mexico in May, 1944.
   — Ross Collection

The Keller Crew: From left, standing: Stan Levine, Walter R. Ross, George F. Keller, Eugene Correll, Jr. , Carl Holden. Kneeling from left: Martin L. Zapf, Gerald Blake, Christine Nikitas, Robert M. Conley, Shelby Fowler, and Travers Harman.
— Ross Collection

Scenes of headquarters and living quarters of 9th Bomb Group at Tinian.
— Ross Collection

𝔗his is to certify that
CAPT. WALTER R. ROSS
𝔍s a member of the 𝔈aterpillar 𝔈lub whose life was spared the 8th day of AUG., 1945 because of an emergency parachute jump from an aircraft. 𝔐embership certificate has been issued to the end that this safety medium, in the art of flying may be furthered.

5/3/46

....
ISSUED   SECRETARY

Walter Ross looks over memorabelia during commeration of the 25th anniversary of his release from Prisoner of War camp.
— Ross Collection

Picture taken of part of Tom's crew at Tinian in 1945. From left: Walt Ross, John Peterson, Gary Muchnicr, Bob Drew, and Milt Goede.
    — Ross Collection

These buildings were part of the POW camp where the author was interned.
 -Ross Collection

Former Lt. Nobuchi Fukui, far right, with parents and wife and children.
 – Ross Collection

Crosses with inscriptions in Japanese reading, "Tomb of a brave American soldier," are believed to mark the graves of the U.S. servicemen killed when the United States dropped the atomic bomb on Hiroshima. The photograph was given to Walter Ross, a Kansas City businessman, in 1981 by a Japanese TV crew that was doing a report on the bombing and American deaths. While a prisoner of war, Mr. Ross had talked to two Americans who were in Hiroshima when the bomb exploded on August 6, 1945.
— Ross Collection

WESTERN UNION

.PA(52) 46 3 EXTRA GOVT=WUX WASHINGTON DC VIA ALBUQUERQUE NMEX
AUG 29

MRS LUCILLE E ROSS=
    6569 BALMER TER=

THE SECRETARY OF WAR HAS ASKED ME TO EXPRESS HIS DEEP REGRET
THAT YOUR HUSBAND 1/LT ROSS WALTER R HAS BEEN MISSING IN ACTION
OVER JAPAN SINCE 8 AUG 45 IF FURTHER INFORMATION OR OTHER
DETAILS ARE RECEIVED YOU WILL BE PROMPTLY NOTIFIED=

    E F WITSELL ACTING THE ADJUTANT GENERAL OF THE ARMY.

    2/LT 8 45.

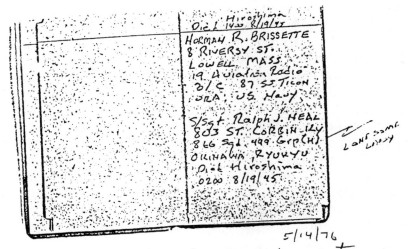

5/14/76

This is to certify that the above Log entry was made by me, Walter R Ross, then Lt. Army AF 01323741 on or about 8/19/1945. Sgt Neal was a P.O.W. in Hiroshima at the time the Atomic Bomb was dropped. He was brought into my camp by the Japanese on or about 8/17/45. I along with my B 29 crew of 10 were also P.O.W.s. Sgt Neal was with me up until his death on 8/19/1945 at 0200. He died from the effects of the Atomic Bomb. His body was removed by the guards and I do not know where he was buried.   Walter Ross

NOTARY PUBLIC STATE OF MISSOURI
MY COMMISSION EXPIRES APR-23-1979

WALTER R ROSS
9616 MOHAWK RD LEAWOOD
KAN 66206

Soon after the planes left we heard a tremendous explosion. We had no idea what could cause such a loud noise[24].

Until today our hearty breakfast had kept us going when we decided to start rationing our food and water. Each person received one candy charm (similar to a life Saver) and a sip of water. We were on our honor. Everyone took just one sip as agreed upon then passed the canteen around to the next person in an orderly fashion.

Each man calmly accepted the rations as scheduled without question. Everyone knew what it would take a combined effort to survive, therefore we kept our minds alert and eyes constantly on the lookout for the submarines, always confident that rescue would come.

Carl Holden and Stan Levine kidded me about my saving money. I had practiced being frugal and had accumulated about $5,000.00 a lot of money in those days. "How much would you give up to get rescued? Lucille will sure have a good time on all that money," they said. Their kidding continued for days.

During the night we heard planes and took a chance that they were friendly and shot off flares, but we did not attract their attention.

The night was clear, but again the moon remained very dark. There was no light except for the bright twinkling stars. All that I could see of the men were their silhouettes. They were like black ink against a black painting.

Day Three (Friday)

The following day, August 10, 1945, we decided to increase the rations to one candy charm and one sip of water from twice a day to three times a day. The sweetness of the candy only increased our desire for

---

[24]Following WWII I learned that Nagasaki had also been destroyed by the second atom bomb, named Big Bertha on August 9, 1945. Looking back, I realized that from our position in the Sea of Japan the loud noise we had heard was the explosion of the atomic bomb dropped on Nagasaki.

more water which did not help matters. The wind that blew up in the early morning slightly changed the course of drift. The wind began to kick up the ocean. Small waves developed, which caused some of the ties between rafts to break.

That night, I saw flying phosphorous fish for the first time. I became extremely frightened seeing them fly out of the darkness and disappear into the black water. At first, I did not know what they were. They appeared over and over again, sometimes crossing right in front of us. I wondered aloud if it was the enemy. "No, they're just phosphorous fish," came a reply from someone who knew.

As the sun set, we witnessed a sliver of moon low on the western horizon. Correll called it "a cresent moon." In addition, we witnessed many shooting stars. All of this activity broke up the routine of just sitting, day after day, night after night.

Day Four (Saturday)

At midday, we spotted four Japanese planes coming toward us from the west at a high altitude. We avoided being seen by covering ourselves with blue tarps, which were included in the rafts. These must have blended with the blue ocean since the planes flew by without seeing us. Perhaps these were the ones we had heard during a previous night. Since they were enemy planes, we were lucky they had not see our flares.

With the passing of time, my skin became painfully sunburned. My lips cracked, split open and bled. I had such fair skin, some people called me Whitey. I was so blistered they could have called me Patches. Talking became a way to pass the time, always about food and sitting in a bath tub of ice and drinking whatever. Even sex entered the conversation. Unshaven, our beards grew scratchy and irritated my skin. Some of the younger men were surprised they could grow beards. We kidded about these young men, almost boys, to keep each other's spirit high.

Up until now the waves were gentle swells but on this day when the wind came up the water started to churn. Swells increased to about eight feet. We were lucky no one got sea sick, but the rough water added to our misery. The shoelaces holding the rafts constantly broke as the rafts rose up and down on the waves.

Each time this happened, the rafts separated. Although we were losing strength, we paddled hard to keep us together again.

As waves came over the sides, I tried scooping the water out of my raft using my cupped hands. More water splashed in than I was able to scoop out, but I persevered and kept the raft afloat.

Since rations were depleting fast, we decided to try our luck at fishing with the gear provided in each raft (lines, hooks and cloth bait). Each man bragged that he was a fisherman. We gave each man the opportunity to prove his bragging. Fish were all around us. There were even flying fish. We hoped that one would land in the rafts. As each man failed to make a catch another took his place. Those of us who fished leaned over the side while remaining seated. It was impossible to stand on the wobbly bottom of the raft. We were in no hurry, not going anywhere, so we continued for hours.

There was not a fisherman amongst us. Then, we tried spearing the fish with make shift spears, using our pen knives with no luck. We then turned to shooting gulls with pellets also included in our equipment.

Having qualified as an expert on the firing range, the task fell on me. Maybe because I was a bird watcher before joining the service or because the raft kept bobbing up and down and the birds flew an erratic flight pattern, but in either event, I could not hit one. I do not know what we would have done with it if we shot one; we did not have to make that decision. I was neither a fisherman nor a hunter. We reluctantly returned to rationing one charm and one sip of water each, three times during the day. The menu was getting old fast. The sweet candy continued to increase our craving for more and more water. It was becoming a real problem.

So as not to be too heavy on any one person, the two men riding on laps continued to rotate on a regular basis but at shorter intervals. Riding on top became more difficult at night, especially when the man on top fell asleep and keeled over into the black water. Someone would yell, "Man overboard!" We would awaken in a daze, our skin begged for relief, but in the black of the night, we would grapple for the man. It took a lot of time before we all got back to sleep. I'm not sure everyone slept at the same time.

    I knew I was losing weight and stamina. It took all I could muster to get myself back into the raft each time I fell overboard. The other men had to grab me by the seat of my pants to hoist me in. Without their help, I'm not sure I could have made it. My legs would go numb when someone was riding on top of me, I wasn't certain I could take it much longer. The longer we drifted the more often we rotated. Each time we hauled someone in, more water came into the rafts with him, dragged in by his wet clothing. We could never get dry. It took a lot of effort scooping the water out with our cupped hands, just to keep afloat. As our strength rapidly decreased, it became increasingly more difficult to lift each man out of the cold water and back into the raft. These conditions continued day after day without relief. My salt water sores ate my flesh. With each salty spray, the water stung the sore. My skin cracked and bled. I could run my hand along the midsection of my body and feel the painful dents where my clothing had rubbed away the skin.

    The men were so tired, they fell into the water more frequently. The ties binding our rafts together had been knotted and reknotted so that little remained to the ties. The ocean waves constantly rose and fell, straining the thinning strands of lace.

    Our biggest problem came at night when one of the men fell soundlessly into the water, or we were too tired to notice a raft had broken free and slowly drifted from the group. "Man adrift," someone would yell as he noticed a raft was missing.

    Each time we became more panicked, uncertain whether we had the energy to paddle as a unit to bring him back to our unit. Finally, we tried holding onto each others hands, but when we fell asleep our grip released and the raft drifted away into the black of the night.

By now the crew had been together for more than eight months through many good and difficult times, but now we were being tested to really work as a team. We were alive, only because we depended on others to rescue us. The three people who gave up their rations did not complain or request that they get a bigger share of the daily distribution. I had little or no commanding to do.

Eventually, we began functioning as a democracy. No one would take more than his share of the rations and would contribute as much as possible toward our survival. We talked out our situation whenever a question arose. In the past the pilot did not have much commanding to do. Each man knew his responsibility on the plane and went about doing his job. This same attitude prevailed. It just made my job easier. I noticed a real bond and trust developing among the men.

Holden continued to wish he had more time at piloting the plane. I agreed. I felt it would have been better had Holden had more experience. Perhaps this would not have happened.

This night the cresent moon became visible earlier and higher in the western sky and more than just a sliver.

Day Five (Sunday)

"Land ho, land ho!" someone shouted as dawn broke. On August 12th, I could see for the first time that we were drifting toward land. It was barely visible to me but the thought of getting onto land was sufficient enough to get us extremely excited.

By this time I did not have any idea of our location, since we had been drifting for four days in what appeared to be in a northeasterly direction. As the sun rose higher in the sky, the land began to look more like an island. We thought it was not big enough to be Honshu, Japan's biggest island, it must be just a small island. "This could be a break for us," I said. "A small island might be easier to sneak onto. Fewer people to hide from." Although the faint island seemed very, very far away, we decided to start paddling towards it. Everyone grabbed a paddle and started paddling.

Our supplies were almost nil, so I decided, since we did not know how long it would take to reach land fall we should reduce the rations from three times a day to twice a day. I gave each man one charm and one sip of water for each rationing period.

When a gas tank floated past us, we all got excited and shouted, "We must be near civilization." We continued our paddling until about 2 a.m. when, completely exhausted, we just had to stop. The moon continued to become larger and brighter as it neared its one-quarter phase. We continued locating the North Star and constellations. I could see the strength leaving each man, our food could not sustain this effort much longer.

Day Six (Monday)

At dawn, August 13, 1945, the sunrise again gave me a short lived joy. We soon discovered that during the balance of the night we had lost distance by drifting back away from land caused by an off shore wind. The struggle renewed. We had to make up the lost distance.

The wind increased, and aggravated our sunburned faces all the more. Our lips cracked open and bleed. We had no medication for our skin, no hats to relieve the sun's relentless heat.

We knew the typhoon season was approaching so each clear day was a welcome sight. Seeing the darkness of the night fade away gave me a certain amount of comfort. Not being able to see anything at night was scary to me. I was as concerned about sharks as I was about starvation.

With food and water almost depleted we decided to make an all-out effort to paddle as hard as possible to reach land by nightfall. The plan was to slip ashore, gather some food and water and to go back to sea and wait for the submarines. Never once did we doubt our rescuers were trying to find us.

It took a lot of pushing and driving to keep everyone paddling. Our energy was almost gone. We were sleeping more and talking less.

Our first real confrontation started on our sixth day at sea, when Shelby Fowler, the flight engineer, started to complain that our forward progress toward shore was not working. He complained, "Trying to keep eight rafts together is unruly. We need to separate into four rafts each. A smaller group has a better chance of sneaking on shore and getting supplies without being seen."

I vetoed his idea of breaking up our forces. "I want us to remain together. There is more strength in numbers." For the moment the case was closed, everyone carried on.

With our candy Charms gone, we changed our menu to chocolate bars. They had been held back in reserve from the C-1 vests, for just this moment. The bars were packed in a tin to preserve them and needed to be cut into small portions for each of two meals, also the length of each sip of water was shortened.

Each time a man sipped, we counted out loud, "One thousand one, one thousand two," etc.

Our paddling came to an abrupt halt at about 0300 on the morning of the 14th. Exhausted, we had to stop to rest for the balance of the night, regretfully without making our goal to reach land. We just could not go on any more without a rest stop. The moon was brigher this time and higher in the sky. Correll said, "We should be seeing the full moon on August the 23rd."

The men only moaned. "We hope we won't be out here that long." The island must have been much further away than originally thought.

Day Seven (Tuesday)

I felt the glow of the rising sun on my face as it awakened me. Again, it was a welcome sight because of possible storms during this season. Typhoons, as hurricanes are called in this region, could come at almost any time in August and September. This was my constant fear. I knew we would not be able to sustain high winds and rough seas. As the light of the day increased we soon observed, to our dismay, that once again we had drifted away from land. The good news was that we were closer to the land than at the beginning of the previous day. Encouraging to say the least. "Paddle. Paddle." I ordered, which continued until about noon when a light wind blowing toward land came up. This was a welcomed wind. We broke out sails from the life rafts. The sea got just a little more choppy than the day before, but with the breeze to our back, the sea was relatively smooth for sailing. Fowler kept insisting we divide into two. "Progress is too slow," he said. Reluctantly, I agreed.

Holden said, "You should not make this decision." He felt that Fowler's action was breaking up our unit. We had been doing well up until now. "Why change?"

But, as he said, we were having such difficulty keeping all the rafts tied together and holding eight rafts in a straight line while under sail. Before breaking up into two groups we divided our remaining water supply. We did not have any more food to distribute. The final rations had been distributed earlier in the day: one chocolate bar divided into 10 portions for breakfast and dinner, one swallow of water. All that remained were bouillon cubes which we reluctantly broke into pieces and tried to swallow without water. To this day I can still taste the salty lump I tried to get down and can remember the horrible feeling of trying to swallow my dry portion, it tasted terrible.

Now with four rafts we were able to hold our course. Fowler's group seemed to make better progress than my group and got considerably farther ahead. I guess he had a point to prove. As it turned out, both floats made better headway after breaking into two groups.

By this time our optimism was waning. The Navy must have had plenty of time to arrive. I will say this, "our group was optimistic and continued to talk about a cold drink and a steak even though our situation looked so bleak." Disappointed, I finally acknowledged the Navy would not rescue us.

In light of our discovery, separating was the right thing to do. I wondered if one group would be rescued, and the other stranded. What would happen to the crew who reached land first, if they reached land at all. It was getting harder for me to make rational decisions. We were in a tenuous situation, to say the least.

CHAPTER 10

Taken Prisoners of War

The Capture

We released the last of our energy, paddled with the wind to our backs, and pushed ourselves forward until about 1900 hours (7 p.m.) on August 14, 1945. The first of our two groups had advanced to within 200 or 300 yards of land. As Fowler and his four rafts came closer and closer toward the beach, they were spotted by Japanese fishermen. The Japanese quickly launched four motor fishing boats and were coming out to intercept them.

Meanwhile, the sail we had hoisted on the lead raft was catching the wind nicely while everyone paddled as hard as possible. I thought about out-running the fishermen, and trying to land farther down the island beach, but we were too exhausted. There was no doubt we would be captured. We had no food, no water. How much worse could things get? Our planes had given up on us, we never saw a submarine, so the likelihood of help appearing at this very moment was remote.

As our distance closed I could see that the first group had already been taken as prisoners of war. From past stories and accounts about the treatment of Americans captured by the Japanese, I feared for our lives.

With our capture imminent, we talked about our side arms. Finally, we all agreed that since we did not have the strength or numbers to fight and win, it would be safer to be captured without our pistols. Reluctantly we slid them into the water.

Two of the fishing boats started toward shore with our first group, but they were too far away by this time for me to observe how my men were being treated. The other boats came toward us. I thought, as I watched, "After all our struggles for seven days, it all comes down to this."

It was early evening of our seventh day at sea by the time the Japanese fishermen reached us.

The decision by each crew member to throw away his side arms (pistols) turned out to be a good one. The fishermen were as hospitable as possible under these circumstances. They pulled up alongside of us and hauled each man aboard, pulled all of our gear on deck, then gave us cigarettes and as much water as we could drink (from what appeared to be saki bottles). Blessed are the merciful.

We were not tied up or blindfolded. They could not speak English, but by hand signal motioned us to be seated on the deck. We just sat there completely dazed wondering, what was in store for us and how we would be treated? What could be worse than the torture we'd already endured? All these questions remained unanswered as we headed toward shore. The fishermen did not appear hostile. My guess is they sensed we were of no threat to them. Exhausted, frightened, speechless, we just sat there. We did not learn until weeks after that we had been floating in mined waters and that neither submarine nor air patrol could rescue us.

Encounter with the Enemy

We reached a small fishing village at about 2000 hours, having no idea where we were. The other group remained in their boats while the villagers swarmed all over them. As we docked we were met by a group of villagers which by this time had grown into a large body of hostile people. The fishermen kept us on their boats while the villagers clambered on board. "Americans!" they shouted, kicking the sides of the boat, beating us with large sticks. One man who looked like a member of the military smashed his large stick down onto my wrist, which split the skin wide open. Blood trickled down my wrist and down to my fingers. A huge gash opened between my thumb and wrist. Women threw rocks at us. Children gathered spiders and shoved them down the back of our necks.

I could tell by their clothing that the villagers were workers, farmers and fishermen. They had on what looked like American pajamas. Nothing fancy. I did not see any colorful kimonos. They all wore straw hats with large brims. Some ladies wearing long dresses carried babies. All of the children wore pants with their shirts hanging out.

They came at us by the hundreds, yelling, leaping angrily above the crowd, hungry to retaliate. They spit on us, screamed, sneered with such a frenzy, their voices seemed to build on each other.

Spiders crawling down my back seemed to slide through my sweat. I had no way of knowing how many times I would be bit, or if I'd even survive their poison.

We did not have the energy to fight back, although I thought, "It is useless; the odds are against us." I sensed the futility of such an action on our part. We huddled together, our heads bowed, terribly humbled by the hatred towards us. Escape was furthermost from our minds. I thought, "How does an American hide?" Even if successful, it would be impossible to go back out to sea.

We politely asked for someone who could speak English and requested that the military be informed of our presence. One man in uniform stepped forward. He appeared to be from the home guard. He took charge and saw to it that we were removed from the boats.

Villagers shoved sticks into our backs, whacked us over the shoulders with tree limbs. They threw rocks at our heads and tossed sand into our faces. We could hardly walk from weakness and mistreatment. Some villagers assisted us to the beach where all of our gear had been piled. They pulled our Mae West life jackets and C-1 vests off and threw them onto the pile. Even though it was a short distance from the fisherman's boat to the beach I felt the pain in my legs from being cramped into the life rafts. I had no idea just how weak I was until then. I stumbled several times as I tried to stand. Through it all the crew helped each other. The walk to the beach was only about 100 yards but the constant harassing, the hitting, the sand throwing, all added to our misery of walking. It seemed to take forever to reach the area where our gear had been piled.

As darkness approached confusion reigned. It had been a big day for the villagers of this remote place to capture American fliers and they were making the most of it. The villagers crowded in a circle around us. They shoved and pushed each other, trying to get as close as possible. Some of them carried lighted flame torches even though total darkness had not fallen.

The children continued harassing us. I felt inhuman being beaten. Several gruff men pushed us to the ground and tied our hands behind our backs. The civilians never let up harassing us by throwing rocks, sand. The women and children hit us with long poles. The children scurried for more spiders to shove down our shirts.

Suddenly, members of the Japanese armed services (army or navy or home guard) arrived in uniform carrying rifles. The officers wore Samurai swords. After they finished placing our equipment in front of us, they forced us to kneel in a line and bow our heads.

I glanced at the knees of the men on either side of me, thinking I should remember who was beside me when I died. One of the officers ran the back of his cold, shiny silver Samurai sword across the back of each of our necks. It sent the civilians into a wild cheer. He gave a long speech to the villagers speaking Japanese. He probed at us with his long sword as he spoke. I was sure he was waiting for the right moment to decapitate us all.

When he placed the sword's blade across the back of my neck, I felt a twinge run through my stomach, and

I almost wet my pants. I waited for blood, but there was none. His sword had not penetrated my skin.

The villagers cheered him on, reminding me of the old westerns when everyone turned out to watch a hanging.

My mind immediately flashed back to scenes I had witnessed in the news clips at the movies of Japanese beheading servicemen taken on Bataan and Corrigidor. Being the bombardier, I wondered, "Would they search me out? Would I be the first?" I was located in the middle of the line.

If I was not executed first, how could I stand to see the bodies of my buddies fall forward beside me? Who amonst us would feel the most pain? I wondered how Lucille would learn about my death.

The guards reached into our pockets and removed personal items. Many of these items had sentimental value since they had been given as gifts by grandparents, wives or sweethearts when we enlisted in the service. These items were never recovered[25].

And then, one of the Japanese officers brought a bucket to the line and took out a dipper of the contents. He presented it to the first crewman in line, who refused his offer. The second in line took a sip only to learn that it was water. When the first man asked for some the officer whacked him on the head with the ladle for refusing. He then gave each of us a drink then went back and gave the first man a drink. The Japanese officer proceeded to make his final talk to the civilians before moving us. At the conclusion he ordered his soldiers carrying rifles to blindfold us and get us onto our feet. The soldiers bound us together in a long line and led us away from the beach up a long dirt hill. Most of us had removed our shoes for ease in swimming or to use the laces to tie the rafts together. Now, without shoes, our walk up a rocky road became very painful. Being blindfolded made it impossible to miss walking on the

---

[25]Later on while in P.O.W. camp I made a list of the jewelry and personal effects they removed from us. See Appendix H page 172

rocks and sharp articles on the road. My feet must have curled around every rock along the way. Whenever we faltered or fell the soldiers beat us with the butt of their rifles and yanked on the rope to get us up. They beat us at will. The soldier's constant jerking on the ropes that bound us together added to the difficulty of walking.

As I fell to the ground I remembered a motion picture in which Jesus Christ was carrying His cross up the hill. Each time He fell to His knees a Roman Centurion whipped His bare back with his leather whip of many strands. For the moment, I could feel for Him. Each time He faltered, He got up. I tried to do the same. I felt the pain on my bare feet and the butt of the rifle striking my head. I stumbled, and someone jerked the rope that bound me, forcing me to get up.

After what seemed to be about three or four miles of walking, we arrived at some sort of military post. I could see the compound by peeking under my blindfold. It was here that we met more Japanese troops and an officer who spoke English. We all sat huddled together while some of the crewmen were untied and led to a room for interrogation.

I sat on the wet sandy soil for the remainder of the night. Whenever I went to sleep and fell over, the guards would give me a whack on the head with the butt of his rifle until I sat up. Knowing that I would receive a blow to the head if I feel asleep, I was caught between that fear, and the need to get some rest. I was so tired. Hearing the same actions being done to others was nerve racking. The kicking and beating continued until day break. I felt helpless and degraded, treated poorly as an unruly dog.

During the early hours the soldiers began constructing some sort of platform. Our navigator, while returning from his interrogation session, reported seeing a large knife swinging from a rope above some baskets. He also saw soldiers lining baskets with straw. In our present state of mind, I imagined our heads rolling at the edge of a blade, dropping into the basket. We all knew how the Japanese treated P.O.W.s in Bataan and Corregidor. Fear washed over me each time a crew member was taken away for interrogation by the Japanese English-speaking interpreter.

I was lucky not to be called out for interrogation. I was scared enough without going through that routine and my crew was careful not to divulge rank. As each man returned he tried to whisper the scene that took place. We huddled together, never knowing who was next to us at any given moment. If they heard us speak, we were hit on the head by a rifle butt. I wanted to calm the men, but we would all get hit if we said anything.

Since the U.S. had air superiority we had been instructed prior to our mission to give any information asked during interrogation if we were taken prisoners. During the sessions they asked one question like "How many planes does U.S. have?" Another question they wanted to know was, "How many women did each crew carry on the plane?" Apparently they thought we had all the comforts of home.

In the morning, at the edge of dawn, I peered under my blindfolds and saw soldiers hanging panels, flags, and banners on ropes strung up across the front of the building and behind the platform. It looked like a celebration was about to take place. My imagination ran rampant and I visualized being used for target practice. In my weakened state I could imagine just about anything.

In the middle of the interpreter's questions, he was interrupted and called away. "What is going on?" we asked each other. This delay was nerve racking to me. Each little action on their part set off our wildest imagination of torture. While he was away the warm sun came up and all of the military personnel suddenly let out with some sort of chanting. It went on and on. I suppose it had something to do with their religion or paying homage to the Emperor. I fantasized it was a ritual before our execution.

The soldiers continued to chant while they formed a circle around us while carrying their rifles. We continued to think the worst. Perhaps we were about to be used for bayonet practice. I did not know what to expect, only speculation as the chanting and circling continued. We huddled next to each other, and said our goodbyes. We were no longer panicked, only resigned. Being so exhausted, we just sat, bound together, silently.

Finally, the chanting stopped when the interpreter returned. The silence was deafening. He lined the crew up and marched us under guard to a local train station where we were to board a train. Leaving this place relaxed me a little. I had survived another day. All of that speculation was for naught, but the fear was real. While waiting for the train, the guards formed an armed circle around us to protect us from the angry crowd that had assembled at the station. As their numbers increased along with their hostility, it was all the guards could do to hold them back.

The angry crowd pushed closer and closer. The guards (soldiers) tightened their circle around us and told us to lay down on the ground. Through my blindfolds, I watched the soldiers hold their rifles at chest height to restrain the civilians.

Then word came down from their commanding officer to board the train. The crowd gave way while continuing shouts of anger at us. Blindfolded, I could feel their angry breath on my back. The breeze blew by me as they whacked the air, trying to reach me.

Before boarding the train our navigator Lt. Correll gave his gold second lieutenant bar to a Japanese soldier in exchange for some water which he shared with the crew. After a few sips we learned that it was hot weak tea. It was the first refreshing drink since receiving some from the officer at the beach.

Just as we were about to board the train there was complete silence. Then we hear someone giving what appeared to be a speech over the loudspeaker. Since it was in Japanese we could not understand or tell who was making the speech[26]. After the speech, we continued boarding the train.

While inside the train I could not sense any hostilities among the passengers. Since I could not see them I had to imagine their behavior, but I could feel their presence surrounding me.

I found the ride most uncomfortable since I was not able to lean back because my hands were tied behind me. After a short ride, we arrived at the town Iwakuni while we were loaded into the back of a truck.

My ride in the back of the truck became very degrading to me. In order to get into the truck they removed the ropes around our wrists but kept us blindfolded. I had to urinate so badly I could not hold it any longer. I knew there was a guard on board so with hand and arm signals I was able to communicate with him by pointing toward my fly. After getting his attention he stopped the truck and guided me to the railing and nudged me to go over the side of the truck. I got the picture. I felt like an animal, blindfolded, not knowing who was watching.

After arriving at what appeared to be a military headquarters, we were marched up three exhausting flights of stairs and permitted to remove the blindfolds before we sat on the floor. This was our first exercise in days and we felt it in our leg muscles. As each man had his blindfold removed, I saw the fear in each of their

---

[26]On August 14, a single B-29 snowed leaflets over Tokyo apprising the startled people of the negotiations . The Emperor heard differing opinions of this hostility and convened the cabinet. But the final arguments had been delivered at Hiroshima and Nagasaki. The Emperor spoke. His people must suffer no longer. The war must end.

This decision crushed the revolt. To oppose the Divine Will was unthinkable. That night the Imperial Government transmitted acceptance of the allied terms and announced to his subjects that their Emperor would broadcast an unprecedented message. Never had an Emperor of Japan spoken directly to his people.

Senso Owari - "The war is over."

Before the revolt was over Lt. Gen. Takeshi Mori, Commander of the Konoye Division, was killed and the Prime Minister Kantaro Suzuki and Privy Council Baron Kiichiro Hiranvma homes were burned.

Source: Beyond Courage by Dorothy Cave.

faces. I saw tired, dirty men bleeding from their lips caused by exposure to the sun as each sat on the floor. I waited on the floor while some of the crewmen were taken away again for further interrogation. For some unknown reason they never picked me.

The stark, dreary looking building consisted of small rooms where some of the crew were taken for their interrogation. Those being interrogated refused to accept cigarettes during the interrogation unless all of the crew members were offered some. Non-smoker's, including me, agreed it became difficult to smoke the ones given to us. I feared they would be insulted if I did not accept the cigarette. I coughed at each puff. Putting on an act of satisfaction was difficult. As the interrogations continued, again I was not singled out.

During our stay and interrogation at Iwakuni headquarters on August 15, 1945, the guards took the balance of our watches, jewelry, etc.

A very young boy we started calling our mascot, brought pails of water and rolls made of rice flour called pan. It was our first food since yesterday when we ate our remaining rations just prior to our capture. After a short rest, we each were given two more rolls.

I had not had a bowel movement since I left Tinian eight days earlier. I guess with the rolls and walking up the flight of steps it triggered the action. The bowel movement was excruciating. The pain was beyond belief. I felt like I was passing my arm. However, following the pain the relief was worth it.

That night, blindfolded and tied, we were marched through town to a jail and all crowded into one cell about 8' x 10' with straw mats on the floor and blankets. Some slept well. After the beatings I took the night before, I was reluctant to sleep. At least here we had the luxury of running water for the first time since leaving Tinian. After seven days of being in salt water and then laying on the dirt and sand on the beach and the dirt in the compound, our bodies and clothing were filthy. Our skin was covered with open salt water sores. Blood was oozing from my lips and waist area. The running water was appreciated and enjoyed and helped to soothe the pain of the bloody open sores. On August 16, 1945, the ninth day following our departure from Tinian, our journey continued, once again tied and blindfolded we were put onto another train. Before boarding and prior to being blindfolded we were given two buns each.

This train ride took us through a city I could see by holding my head in a particular position. I peeked out from under the lower side of the blindfold and saw a city totally destroyed. I observed at the remains of building after building completely leveled. As the bombardier I could easily see how they could place this destruction on me. I bombed many times but never got to see the results first hand. I thought, "Could my bombs have done similar destruction?" I knew it was not Yawata because we had drifted away from there and had not been transported over any large bodies of water after our capture. We had to be on Honshu, the largest island in Japan. I thought maybe this was the city we heard about that had been bombed by a new type of bomb. The charred rubble made it difficult for me to identify anything. As the train slowed I saw area after area where nothing was left standing, except for partial pieces of concrete columns, a few brick fireplaces and chimneys, some small curls of smoke rose from the ashes.

I could not see any people. My viewing scope was limited but it appeared that no vehicles were moving, only desolation. Silence. That is all I could see as our train slowly pulled into the train station which appeared to be the only partially destroyed building still standing. Apparently the tracks had been cleared sufficiently to permit the train to pass.

After detraining, soldiers with rifles marched us a short distance and threw us to the ground. The ground was bare and rough. Because there were no buildings standing to house us we just laid out on the open ground in a revetment, exposed to the elements.

The sun was very hot as we laid there thirsty and hungry, occasionally receiving a drink of water. The guards permitted us to move into a shadow cast by one of the few partially standing structures which gave us some relief from heat of the day.

As night fell, we tried to sleep on the dirt, while being plagued by vicious mosquitoes. The movement of the guards, who always seemed to be celebrating, disturbed me. I guess I felt that way because of my plight. Being dirty, hungry and scared made it easy for my mind to wander. "When will the execution take place?"

Neal and Brissette

The next day, August 17th, guards brought in two American aviators and threw them to the ground in front of us. Both men lay helplessly. Their mouths hung open, expressing great pain. They found it difficult to communicate with us, but we were able to get their names and some sketchy information. They said they were Ralph Neal and Norman Brissette.

As the day went on Brissette said, "I had been a gunner on a Navy dive bomber flying off the aircraft carrier Ticonderoga." Then Neal spoke, "I was a replacement ball gunner on the B-24 named the Lonesome Lady flying from Okinawa. My machine gun had been removed to conserve weight, making me a gunner without a gun." He continued, "I was not a regular member of the crew." Their target had been the Battleship Haruna harbored at the Kure naval dockyards, a mission which took place on July 28, 1945.

I could see from under my blindfold they were slowly dying a very horrible death. It appeared that their injuries were more than from beatings. They vomited frequently. The parts of their bodies that were exposed were covered with running sores and bruises. They did not have the energy to shoo away the flies that walked freely in and out of their open mouths.

Both men spoke incoherently about their planes being shot down. One recalled after they released their bombs they turned away from their target. Their flight plan took them, they thought, in the direction of Hiroshima[27] as they headed back to their home bases.

After realizing their planes were on fire the crews of both planes bailed out, not knowing if the anti-aircraft fire that hit them came from the area around the target or later on by the battery located in Hiroshima. Neal said, "My tail gunner, Abel, bailed out from the rear of the plane and the rest of the crew went out the front of the plane.

"Upon reaching the ground we were captured and rounded up with others from three planes, 13 in all, and taken to a place that looked like a castle." There they joined twelve other prisoners making a total of 23 Americans beening held in this camp.

They explained, "During the early hours one morning a bomb hit our P.O.W. camp and totally destroyed all of the buildings. Fire was everywhere. Surviving guards ran in all directions. All of our fellow P.O.W.s were killed except us. We managed to get free of the burning buildings and jumped into a cesspool, exposing only our noses in order to breathe, as the flames burned all around us. We remained submerged until the fire burned out. As we climbed out we were immediately recaptured by soldiers. On our way to this location the guards and surviving civilians beat us severely."

They had no idea as to where their camp was located or the type of bomb that killed the other P.O.W.s. All they knew was that their camp had been completely destroyed by this bomb and that they were the only survivors. Neal said, "My pilot, Tom Cartwright had been taken from the camp a few days earlier and sent

---

[27]The Japanese troops based in Hiroshima were battle ready for any plane coming their way and set their sights on the planes leaving Kure. Anti-aircraft guns bracketed the B-24 Taloa and brought it down. Then the Lonesome Lady came over and appeared to be on fire, perhaps from the guns at Kure. It was heading toward the battery of guns near Hiroshima Castle. They open fired on it. Prior to crashing into the mountain side, the crew bailed out. Source: <u>Enola Gay</u> by Thomas and Witt.

away, I think to Tokyo for interrogation." Neal told us, "I never saw Abel or Cartwright again."

As the day went on I tried to sleep with both men laying on the ground helplessly in front of me. Pus oozed from their ears. I continued to feel that their condition was caused by more than from their severe beatings, but I had no way of knowing differently. They were incapable of helping themselves. I felt badly that I did not have the strength or the wisdom to assist them.

Meeting Lt. Fukui/The Christian[28]

On the evening of August 17, 1945, a Japanese lieutenant who spoke English presented himself to us as Lt. Fukui. Looking from under my blindfold I saw a stocky built, short, neatly dressed officer carrying a Samurai sword. He said he was a Christian and felt the urge to help the American prisoners. He informed us that we were going to be moved. Fukui also told us that his Christian parents lived in Dartmouth. He explained that in Japan a person can have two sets of parents; one who gave birth and the other set, their teachers. It was for this reason he made mention of his Christian parents in the United States when he first met us. He said, "I am going to try to secure safe passage for you," and would return when he obtained it. When he used the words "safe passage" fear gripped me again. With all the activity going on in the background I just knew the day of our execution had arrived. Looking back, I can see how my mind was denying his kindness.

Before he departed he said, "Japan had signed the International Prisoner Treaty to treat prisoners warmly. With that, I am going to meet with my colonel to secure necessary papers for your safe passage."

---

[28]Following the Meiji period (1868) Christianity was once again permitted in Japan and the Catholics with their success in the 16th century continued. The European and American Protestant missionaries who came to Japan (1869) following the opening of Japan's doors competed with the Japanese Christians. By 1945, however only about 1% of the population had converted to Christianity. Source: "Japan" by Martin Hirolemann and Francis King. (Fukui was among this 1%.)

Following Fukui's departure the guards began having a drinking party. We could hear the sounds of rifles and our fears increased once more. Shortly thereafter, a Japanese lieutenant appeared, who we thought was Lt. Fukui returning. We questioned him as to when we would be taken away. In English he replied, "You are not going anywhere. You are staying right here." His voice, and his apparently sudden change in attitude confused us.

As we laid on the open ground waiting Fukui's return, a kind elderly woman appeared, who spoke English, translated our needs to the guards. She came with water and food and gave us, including Neal and Brissette, a drink. She lifted their heads to help them drink because they were incapable of holding a cup. Her food included rice balls and pickled horse radish, a real treat. Neal and Brissette laid there helplessly while their condition seemed to worsen. It was an unpleasant sight to watch the flies gather around them as the amount of pus increased, especially knowing they were once healthy servicemen.

Fukui finally returned under the cover of darkness, and put us onto the flat bed of his truck.

Fukui said, "I presented my case and have been given safe passage for you."

First to Enter Hiroshima

"One bomb, one bomb did all this."

Japanese Lt. Fukui

In our weakened condition we had a hard time assisting Neal and Brissette who were nearly dead. They found it difficult to move their bodies. It took all the energy we could muster to raise them high enough to slide them onto the truck.

After driving a short distance, Fukui stopped the truck and ordered, "Stand up." "Take off your blindfolds," and began giving his lecture. "Look how inhumane the Americans were. One bomb. One bomb," he shouted, "did all this destruction." Saying again,

"Look how inhumane[29] the Americans were, 150,000 died from one bomb." We were in no position to counter, but to ourselves whispered, "How about Pearl Harbor?" and "It looked like someone was playing with matches." Others, "How about Bataan and Corregidor?" Another person said in a low voice, "10,000 American and Filipino soldiers died out of 70,000 on the infamous Death March, is that not inhumane?"

During our tour of the city we learned for the first time that it was Hiroshima. He said, "You are the first Americans to see the city from ground level."

As I viewed the horrors of war, my thoughts flashed back to my preparations for our bombing run on Yawata. In my wildest imagination I could not have envisioned the events and circumstances that would catapult me into the position of being the first Americans to enter Hiroshima after its destruction by the atomic bomb.

While looking over the city I was witnessing the results of the bombing we had heard about on our radio while on our way to bomb Yawata. Unfortunately, we had gotten there before any other American troops, not our plan, but that is the way our mission ended.

The place looked like a giant steam roller had rolled over it, like a vacant lot in the U.S. when all of the buildings had been torn down and then bulldozed. I was viewing what remained of a city destroyed by an unknown bomb, to me. There was no noise, not even a dog barking, not a sound, only quiet. Silence. There were no people. No fires, except one here and there. Nothing green. Just complete desolation as far as the eye could see in the darkness of night. There was destruction everywhere.

---

[29]Military planners estimated the invasion of Japan would cost over one million American lives, to say nothing of Japanese troops and civilians, and almost certainly would guarantee the death of every P.O.W. in Japan, Manchuria and Korea. In view of the indiscriminate Japanese bombings of civilians as early as 1932 in China, it is ironic that the Japanese government protested these inhumane bombings of their population. Source: <u>Beyond Courage</u>.

As I witnessed the destruction of Hiroshima, I said, "Walter, you don't know much about military strategy but if the Air Force had used the same number of planes (800) used on Air Force day (August 1) and armed each one with this type of bomb, we could have knocked out 800 cities in one fell swoop, quickening the end of the war."

Ujima

Fukui drove us to the Ujima military police (M.P.) headquarters in the south area of the city. When we reached the station, Lt. Fukui hid us by placing us in what looked like animal cages with bamboo bars within the MP station. The cells were about 10'x10' with bare floors and no furniture. Two of us were put in each cage. Prior to that, we were permitted to go outside to wash up at a pump in the court yard. By now we were again filthy dirty, and still suffering from bleeding lip sores and sores around our waist. The clean water was a welcome treat, making us feel more human. After entering our cells, we were given canned mandarin oranges with chopsticks and a shot of whiskey and permitted to settle in for the balance of the night.

Neal and Brissette continued to get worse. I could hear them moaning and groaning louder and louder, it was getting to me. I had hidden a first aid kit in the leg pocket of my flight suit, which had been overlooked during the search by the guards. I was reluctant to use this morphine on a person with a head injury, fearing I would kill him. I spent a number of agonizing moments before deciding not to use it. A doctor was brought in, who questioned us about the types of medicine to use, so he could use it on the population of Hiroshima. The doctors called the sickness Genshibaku Dansha, the atomic bomb sickness.

Since we had no knowledge of radiation or the type of bomb used, we were at a loss to help. The doctors were treating their patients for burns and wounds, not radiation, something new to them. As a result their patients were not getting any better but only dying at a rapid rate. The doctors were frustrated at not being able to help them. Throughout the day and night fires continued as a result of burning corpses. The possible effects of this bomb and the bomb itself had been kept secret from us so we could not assist the doctors.

Our fate was still unknown to us. Meanwhile in our cells, discussions centered around whether to accept or reject Fukui's statement that he was a Christian. We questioned, "Is he trying to help us or were his efforts just attempting to get information? Does he have Christian parents in the U.S.?" Some wanted to believe this, others thought it was a plot. Those who doubted were disturbed at the others for giving in to the enemy. I happened to be one of those who did not believe him.

He continued, "I learned that the Japanese military had captured ten American aviators (he called us the Korean Channel Group because we had been captured in the waters between Japan and Korea) and were holding them in Hiroshima." He said, "I imagined I was hearing the voices of my American parents telling me to help them."

At this point in time the crew members had no way of knowing how the dropping of the atomic bomb had changed the complex of the war. For us the war continued and we contemplated a long internment in a P.O.W. camp.

Still awake at 2200, we were given a meat stew, again with chopsticks. The next day at 0800 and 1200 we were given bags of rice crackers and at 1800 a bowl of rice and a bowl of browned potatoes. At 2000 we were given a shot of whiskey.

Early the next morning, August 19th, following two nights at Ujima, Fukui turned us over to another officer. After his actions of putting us onto the truck at the Ujima Military Police headquarters I never saw him again[30]. His actions were a mystery to us, "Why did he seek out us?"

---

[30]Until my visit with him in Japan in 1983, 38 years later, long after the war was over.

As we prepared to leave the Ujima MP Station, we learned that Neal had died at 0200 on August 19, 1945. Brissette's condition had weakened and had to be left behind. Later on word came to us that he died at 1400 on August 19, 1945. I made this entry into my diary noting both events[31].

Tode Headquarters

By 0630 we left by truck, blindfolded and tied as usual. On route, they untied us long enough to enjoy a few rice crackers and sips of water. The ride was very tiring, stressful and bumpy. At 1500, we arrived at Tode headquarters, formally a boy's military school, now a government headquarters for interrogation. Our blindfolds and ropes were removed. Following washing by a pump, we were given rice balls, fish and cucumbers. Then P.O.W. cards were made out for each person, by a clerk; we were then taken to the attic hayloft of a barn for the night where we slept on straw mats with blankets. We were guarded by two young Japanese soldiers from Los Angeles, who had been educated in San Francisco before being lured back to Japan just before the war started with an offer of receiving a college education. They had photos of New York, Washington and other cities that pictured these cities as totally destroyed. "Why do you continue?" they asked. "You have lost the war." I knew better, and did not buy their line. My opinion was shared by the entire crew.

From Tode, a truck took us to an organized P.O.W. camp named Hiroshima Camp #1, about 35 miles southeast of Hiroshima. The P.O.W. camp was located on the island of Mukaishima, opposite the town of Onomichi. After getting out of the truck and prior to boarding a ferry to the island the officer in charge lined us up and stated that a peace offering was in the

---

[31]Following the war the debate went on with the question, "Did Americans die in Hiroshima?" I knew from my eyewitness account that Americans had died. Neal and Brissette were among the 23 Americans to die as a result of the atomic bombing of Hiroshima. This information became invaluable in verifying these deaths in the making of the documentary film "Killed By the Atomic Bomb" and used to inform Neal and Brissette's parents.

making, trying to give us the impression that the U.S. was giving up, and that we would be going home soon. Men are not supposed to cry but not a clear eye could be seen, we all broke down, tears streamed over our cheeks because prior to this news we had been anticipating if we lived we would have a long stay in P.O.W. camp. We had not had any prior knowledge that the dropping of the atomic bomb had shortened the war and played an important part in saving our lives. We were overjoyed and happy with the expectation of going home. It became a joyous occasion as we embarked onto the small ferry. Riding with us were Japanese passengers who were not hostile but looked on in curiosity during the short trip to the island. From the landing area we were marched down a street to the gates of the prison.

CHAPTER 11

Life in a P.O.W. Camp

Meeting Fellow P.O.W.s

As I entered the gates of the P.O.W. camp on August 20 I heard the cheers of greetings from the prisoners welcoming us. Prior to our arrival, 106 Americans and 75 British prisoners were housed in the prison camp. The British soldiers had been captured at Singapore and the British merchant marines at sea and the waters off Java. The Americans had been captured during the fall of Correidor and Bataan. They had survived the infamous Death March plus the boat trip to Japan on what became known as the Hell Ships. I met one American soldier who had been captured on Wake Island on December 7, 1941. He was not very coherent by this time. Some had survived the sinking of their Hell Ship by American planes. The ships had not been properly marked to identify them as containing P.O.W.s, making it impossible for U.S. fighters to know they were sinking ships holding American servicemen instead of enemy vessels.

Another P.O.W., Major Ralph Townsend Artman from Suffolk, Virginia, a medical officer, and the only U.S. officer in the camp, used his medical skills to keep the men alive by maintaining strict discipline and sanitation practices.

As we surveyed the camp we noticed there were only a few guards remaining. When we asked "Why?" we learned the Emperor had surrendered. This must have been the broadcast we heard on August 15, 1945. We were not told because we learned later those Japanese who did not want to surrender had other plans for us until Lt. Fukui interceded.

News Hungry P.O.W.s

The hearty welcome resulted from the P.O.W.s being starved for news. They had not received any word from the outside world for almost three years. We broke up into small groups to answer their probing questions. This went on for days. Some had been captured in late December 1941 or early 1942, and had no knowledge of the war in Europe. They were astonished to hear about the new weapons, i.e. Sherman tank, new types of bombs, various types of new airplanes, M-1 rifle, raids by B-17 on Europe and the B-29.

After bathing, we had rice and soup. In the afternoon the P.O.W.s shared their razors, for our first shave since August 7. (I knew then that I could grow a beard). Our first meal consisted of a soup with squash, onions and any vegetable on hand, ripe or green, rice, and with or without barley.

The prisoners were also were interested in hearing about how our bombing missions were orchestrated.

We relived events about our plane taking off from Tinian and going into combat. Ours seemed insignificant after what they had gone through, but they listened intently.

The prisoners had seen B-29s fly over their camp during bombing missions, but never any closer than 10,000 feet. Now they wanted to know more about this magnificent airplane, the Boeing B-29 Superfortress.

We gave them as much information as we could remember.

P.O.W. Camp

The camp was laid out in two sections. One section on each side of the town's main street. One side housed the Americans, the other, the British. Major Artman, lived on the British side with the British officers, and since he was the highest ranking officer, he commanded both contingencies. Our crew was split, with the enlisted men going to the American side and the officers to the British side. A high wall surrounded the camp with doors from both sides leading to the street. Constructed at the gate on the British side was a two story structure used as a command headquarters by the Japanese commandant. In order to get from one side to the other it was necessary to pass through the two tall gates and cross the street. The remaining guards continued controlling of the gates, keeping the men in each section separated, except for allowing prisoners from the American side to travel to and from the kitchen during meal time. It was useless for us to try to escape since there was no place to hide and we did not blend in too well with the Japanese population.

As first lieutenant I had the second highest rank in the camp and therefore, became second in command. I was reluctant to assume this position. It did not seem fair to me since other officers had been there for such a long time before me but these became the rules we lived by. Our quarters were like one story dormitories, with each man having a rice mattress to sleep on. At the far end of the British side was the kitchen and a hot tub. In front of the barrack's was an exercise yard with the infamous box. This infamous box was used by the guards to put prisoners into for disciplinary reasons. In this box a prisoner could not stand or lie down making for extremely crammed quarters, and very uncomfortable, especially in the heat of the day.

We did not see any other American Air Force crewmen contained in this prison.

One of the first things we were permitted to do upon our arrival was to paint a sign board on the roof of our barracks. The Japanese commandant supplied yellow paint and straw. We climbed onto the roof and painted a large circle following by an X, then "23 Crew Here", the call letters of the Nip Clipper, then placed straw onto the wet paint to make it more visible.

After being assigned quarters, our roommates pooled their clothing so we would have something to wear. By this time our flight suits were in shambles and needed washing.

In the military prior to WWII, officers were assigned orderlies and since they were operating under these rules we were assigned one. Holden and I were given Pvt. Glen C. Himes from Ridgeway, Pennsylvania; Pvt. Plymale was assigned to Levine and Correll. They took our clothes and washed them. They sure needed it. We met a Pvt. Pote from the Tufts Campus, near Holden's home, where his father was teaching.

We learned some of our duties from the other officers, such as orderly officer, the British equivalent to our officer of the Day, and about other assignments.

I was assigned the duty to pay the men, at four yen to the dollar, for working on the docks as agreed upon by the Geneva Convention.

On August 24 we organized the Americans into a company with two platoons, three squads each. Until then Major Artman was busy serving as medical and camp director. He welcomed our assistance in organizing the Americans. Dinner consisted of baked squash, potatoes with skins, fish, cucumbers, rice, clear soup, Nashi (fruit) and a lime drink. It seemed like a banquet after our meager rations at sea.

During our confinement the guards maintained a watchful eye over us. However, the brutality they had inflicted on the prisoners before our arrival stopped. Every so often the armed guards disappeared for a few hours, returning with a supply of food. Their primary assignment seemed to be the distribution of our food. However, the Japanese commandant continued to be in control. He communicated with Major Artman on a regular basis and demanded strict discipline. I never doubted he was in control and we were his prisoners.

The following day, August 25, we had our first American formation. We ran up an American flag, one hidden by an enlisted man, small, but the feeling was there.

As an Episcopalian, and with most of the Britains members of the Church of England, I worked with them to construct a prayer book and conducted religious services, which they attended with great enthusiasm. They had forgotten the order of service.

Mercy Missions

When the bombing over Japan stopped and hostilities ceased, the 20th Air Force[32] on August 27 began relief missions using B-29s to drop food supplies to the P.O.W.s.

The sign board we painted guided B-29 mercy flights to our camp. They made an excellent target to guide their aim. The planes were a welcome sight to see. Loaded with empty oil drums filled with food, mostly canned goods, candy, gum, cigarettes, etc. (but no matches), the supplies were dropped by parachutes, some colored red, others blue and still others white. As a Boy Scout I remembered the dimensions of the American flag, and I assisted our crew in using these parachutes to construct the largest American flag you have ever seen. Later on we used it during our repatriation parade out of the camp and down to the ferry. Of course we did not know it but on August 29 the War Department notified our families that we were missing in action. That was 21 days after we were shot down.

On September 6, an exciting thing happened. One of the planes dropping supplies was from our own 9th Bombardment group and we identified it as circle X-29, named "Ready Teddy." One of the mercy planes photographed our sign board and notified our next of kin. They did not know how many but they now knew that some of us had survived.

On a few occasions some of the chutes failed to open. Once a free-falling drum went right through the roof of a barrack, almost hitting a man in his bed.

---

[32]From August 27, 1945 to September 20, 1945, 1,066 B-29's took part in mercy missions. 900 Planes completed their round trip from the Marianas to Japan and dropped 4,470 tons of food by 63,000 parachutes to 63,500 P.O.W.'s to 158 camps. Eight aircraft were lost with a sacrifice of 77 airmen. (MacArthur report.)

Another soldier got up to help his buddy when another drum loaded with food went right through his bed. Had he not gotten up he would have been killed. The impact was like an unexploded bomb, making a large hole in the roof. A lucky turn of events that no one was hurt. From then on, we ordered everyone to get into the bomb shelter. No one questioned that decision. Some Japanese homes were also destroyed from free-falling drums. Whenever these drums burst open, food scattered onto the ground over a large area. Dr. Artman ordered us not to salvage this food but to leave it to the Japanese. He warned us that it could be contaminated. Each day the Japanese came to our camp carrying "honey buckets" as they were called. They dipped the buckets into our latrines and placed them at the end of a pole resting on their shoulders. To keep it from splashing they covered the contents of the bucket with straw. They dumped this onto their cultivated fields for fertilizer. He was afraid of our possible sickness, however the Japanese scooped up the food immediately and ate it as quickly as possible. I never learned the outcome of their health condition. It demonstrated to me just how hungry the civilians were.

Neighboring P.O.W. Camp

We learned from the interpreter assigned to us that another P.O.W. prison in our proximity had not received any food drops from the Air Force. So, some of us, including me, acquired a boat and took food to them. The leader of the expedition, an Englishmen warrant officer A. McNeice, a flying officer with the royal air force stationed in Singapore, who had been captured shortly after the start of the war. When we arrived at the other camp, the Japanese officers greeted us and took our party to a geisha house for dinner. I think we were more scared than they. The Japanese officers knew how to act since they were on their home turf and all carried Samurai swords; we were, of course, unarmed. The officers brought in the geisha girls[33] who fed us and poured saki wine and sang. As we left McNeice threatened the commandant, in fluent Japanese, "If you take this food for yourselves and MacArthur learns about it you will be severely punished." They took him seriously and from that time on they did not harass us.

Following the period when the Emperor made his surrender speech (August 15, 1945) and our liberation (September 13, 1945) the commandant continued to supervise the camp but feared for his life upon MacArthur's arrival.

The guards left us pretty much on our own, coming to the P.O.W. camp occasionally to bring supplies and to keep us within the compound, which became more difficult as time went on.

Warehouse

A building used by the navy as a warehouse served as one of the brick walls of our exercise yard. The P.O.W.s successfully dug under this wall and got into the warehouse. One of the items they stole was liquor, potent enough that when lit it would burn like a bunsen burner. When the P.O.W.s drank it they obviously got very drunk causing us to put them into the infamous box. The prisoners hid their excess loot from the warehouse under the floorboards of their barracks. The Japanese commander would make a passive search these items, but with no luck. He told our commanding officer, "I know they are stealing supplies, but I cannot find them. You must tell your men to stop or disciplinary action will be taken."

Brothel

The prisoners in our camp had been forced into slave labor, by being required to work in the shipyard. One of the wildest stories they told me was their erasing

---

[33]Geisha girls are not prostitutes but attired in a heavy silk kimono, with faces painted white surrounded by a wig of shiny black hair. They wore highly lacquered. special geta or clogs on their feet Their purpose in the Japanese culture is to satisfy the men's need for a female listener instead of their wives. As they play, sing and dance they also hear the men talk about their successes and problems.

the positions of the port holes on the side of the ship they were building and redrawing them at another location that would be below water level. They followed behind the Japanese who measured the location of each port hole and indicated where the hole was to be cut by the worker following him. The P.O.W.s stepped in between him before he arrived with his cutting torch and relocated the holes. Their story went on that when the ship went down the slip and into the water. It just kept going and sunk. (A hearsay but so funny).

Under the terms of the Geneva Convention, the prisoners had to be paid for their work, with no way to spend it, they had accumulated a fair amount. One night, some men got drunk on the stolen alcohol and decided to jump over the wall and find a brothel. They bought passage on the local ferry, went into the town of Onomichi, bought out the entire brothel, and caused quite a stir with the Japanese patrons by throwing all of them out. An excited Japanese officer came to me and requested I come into town and return them to the prison. I lead a group of American and British officers to Onaimichi, entered a warehouse, where we met a group of disgruntled Japanese officers in a dimly lighted room seated at a table with stern faces, while holding their Samurai swords in front of them. The officers instructed us to get the men out of the brothel and return them to our P.O.W. camp. We agreed: power was on their side. As we entered the brothel, the half naked girls greeted us and invited us in. Our men laid on sofas with the other girls, while drinking, eating and having a great time. They were enjoying their moment of freedom from being locked up for such a long time. Getting them away from such a pleasant environment took some real persuasion and getting them onto the ferry was a real effort. Those who were the drunkest were put, one at a time, into the not so famous box. Major Artman also gave all of them something he concocted to make them violently sick in the stomach which helped sober them up. (The irony of the sojourn is that some of them contracted venereal disease.)

After the event at the brothel, we informed the commandant that if he wanted us to be MPs, we needed to be armed. He said he needed a letter of authorization from Gen. MacArthur to honor our request to issue arms. We located a typewriter and I participated in writing such an order and signed General MacArthur's name. Accepting the requisition, the Japanese commandant issued three pistols with ammunition to us. I brought mine home as a souvenir. Unfortunately, I heard rumors that souvenirs would be confiscated while going through evacuation. So I threw away the leather holster and strapped the pistol under my armpit. As it turned out, no one attempted to take it away, causing me great disappointment. Disposing of the holster turned out to be all in vain.

Selling Liquor

Our P.O.W.s had more liquor than they could handle from their plunder of the warehouse so they sold some over the wall to the Japanese civilians. They bartered for a live cow. Some of the prisoners came from farms and knew how to butcher it, so we enjoyed a wonderful treat of having some beef for a change. On another occasion, some of the men asked that I join them on another adventure, which I cannot believe to this day that I participated in. We took some cases of liquor over the wall of the prison, secured a boat, and headed to another nearby island. We sold the liquor while drifting offshore to civilians who came out in their boats to do business with us. My share from the sale was 800 yen. I used my share to buy, through an interpreter, a Japanese kimono for my wife, which she has to this day.

Dinner Out

Interpreter Mr. Furatani, who had been educated at Oxford in England, invited some of the officers including me to come to his home for dinner. As our contribution we brought some sugar from the supplies that had been dropped by the B-29s, it became part of the cooking process. We sat on pillows on the floor around a cooking bowl being heated by coals. His wife, dressed in a kimono came into the room on her knees with the food and cooked it in hot boiling oil. Still on her knees, she backed out. Each time she entered or left the room, she came in on her knees and bowed constantly. We used chopsticks to remove the food from the hot oil and put it into our bowls with rice whereupon we broke a raw egg over the rice and cooked beef. In addition to the beef, we had two bowls of mashed potatoes and a piece of whole fish, about six inches long, three separate cups of seasoning for the fish. A bowl of cucumbers thinly sliced, a bowl of white rice, a bowl of clear broth with fish, and mushrooms were also served. Then some tea. The plate of rice with vegetables was held together with seaweed. Later on during the cooking she added the sugar we brought to the pot. As more of the sugar was added to the cooking oil, the food eventually became dessert.

A ritual which is customary in Japan is for the host to present their guests with a gift. Also, it is the custom for the guest to return the favor. We did not realize it at the time but we had accidently followed their custom by bringing a gift, our gift being the sugar. Upon leaving they presented a gift to each of us, mine became a keepsake of a lovely hand painted scroll picturing lovely soft red roses and hand painted writing in Japanese characters[34].

The Poem

The English were in awe of the B-29 as reflected by their following action. The day before we left the P.O.W. camp, the British soldiers, airmen, and merchant marines who had survived this ordeal, presented us with the following poem as a gesture of their gratitude. They were survivors and wanted to let us and the American B-29 crews know their appreciation;

---

[34]It continues to beautify our home; hanging in our living room. I do not know its age but at the time they presented it, it was already old.

The curator of Chinese art at the Kansas City Nelson Gallery identified the characters as Chinese and the writing was a poem.

Japanese can read Chinese. Although the Japanese language is different it is written with Chinese characters. It is like the English language adopting Latin & Greek words. Source: "Japan" by King & Tuttle.

From the R.A.F. Mukaishima.
To the B-29 crew who crashed in their midst so near the end.

Dedicated in gratitude and admiration.

We've watched you pass above us,
    so near and yet so far.
Close as 20,000 feet, yet distant as a star.
So wonder not we watched your flight
    with envy in our eyes,
For us the confines of four walls,
    for you the boundless skies.
And here were we with nought but hope
    and daily growing thinner,
While five miles off were ten free men
    who'd see no rice for dinner.

You were our single concrete sign
    of how the war progressed.
So obviously masters, the hope
    rose within our breast.
T'was evident the Nippon claims
    were naught but empty boasts,
And how the bitter pill disturbed
    the livers of our hosts.
Thus, as the sirens frequently
    through each increased,
So was the venom of guards
    proportionately released.

T'was then we prayed that you'd avenge
    and with a salvo rock,
The furthermost foundation
    of that cursed and hated dock.
But now we've heard about THAT bomb,
    we breathe a grateful sigh,
And think we're mighty lucky
    that you just passed us by.

And now the war is over,
 we know our freedom's due,
To those three-million-and-a-half
 whose battlefield was blue.
They have fought by sea an land,
 in battleships and tanks,
But your's is the greatest glory.
 To you our warmest thanks.
                    Author
                    Peter Thorne
   Signed by each member of the British Contingency[35]

---

[35]The original hangs on my wall in my home. The poem has been part of talks I have made to service organizations and memorial services at our 9th Bombardment Group reunions.

CHAPTER 12

Repatriation

Victory In the Pacific

"This group of roughly 180 American and Englishmen from Singapore, Tinian, and Bataan marched from their prison to the docks in formation behind an American flag they had made themselves.

Their objective was to leave in a first class military manner, in spite of a great deal of non-military treatment.

I was sure proud of them all."

2nd Lt. Carl Holden
Co-pilot, Keller crew

Prior to our liberation, members of the Swedish and Swiss Red Cross team came to our camp to inform us that the war was over and arrangements were being made for our liberation.

"Surrender of Hitler's last ally, Japan, had taken place aboard the U.S.S. Missouri on September 2, 1945, as the 1st Cavalry Division was unloading on Japanese soil for occupation duty. Advance occupation parties had landed at Atsugi field near Yokohama a few days earlier.[36]

General of the Army Douglas A. MacArthur at the formal signing of Japan's surrender aboard the

---

[36]Source: Mark Clutter, VFW Magazine dated September 1985.

U.S.S. Missouri September 2, 1945[37], made the following statements:

> "It is my earnest hope, indeed the hope of all mankind, that from this solemn occasion a better world shall emerge out of the blood and carnage of the past, a world founded by faith and understanding, the dignity of man and the fulfillment of his most cherished wish for freedom, tolerance and justice."

Shortly after the signing of the surrender paper correspondents started interviewing Japanese. One was an enlisted naval correspondent with the first allied forces to enter Tokyo. He writes;

> "On August 6, 1945, the atomic bomb was dropped on Hiroshima. Japan had been defeated, and Americans were the conquerors. I was sent in to interview prisoners of war and during the next six weeks I heard horror stories that remain with me to this day.
>
> We who were expecting a few months earlier to approach the shores of Japan through a rain of bombs and shells arrived as if it were a routine errand[38]."

History of Wars

No other war in history had been won without an invasion of the enemy's territory. This was done in WWII by B-29s bombing cities throughout Japan, with the aid from all branches of service.

---

[37] The 5th Bomb Squadron issued the following bulletin on September 5, 1945;

The last combat mission this organization participated in was August 14 and 15, 1945, to Kumagaya, Japan with no enemy action encountered nor any casualties. Source: Microfilm roll B0067, frame 1207.

[38] On 2 Sept 1945 the 9th Bombardment Group participating in the 20th Air Force display of power in which they put eight hundred B-29's in the air over the U.S.S. Missouri, the second time in the history of war that such a very large task force of "very heavies" was sent over the Empire. Source: Frame number 1215-1226, microfilm roll number B0067, Headquarters, USAF.

The unconditional surrender of the Japanese empire on September 2, 1945, came about after the relentless bombings by B-29s on the Japanese home islands with the crowning blow, the dropping of two atomic bombs, one on Hiroshima and the second one on Nagasaki.

In historical times only one attempt had been made to invade Japan. That effort was made by the Mongols, under Emperor Kublai Kahn, after they had conquered China; however their fleet was destroyed by a storm and their attempt was unsuccessful. Their second attempt also went down in defeat. The first successful landing of foreign troops on Japan took place in 1945 after they had to capitulated to the Allied forces. This successful endeavor was a great victory and morale booster for the U.S.

First Leg Yokahama

On the day we left our P.O.W. camp on September 13, 1945, we had an occasion to use the American flag we had constructed out of the material from the red, white, and blue parachutes used in dropping supplies to us. As we left the prison we formed up on the street between the two camps in orderly fashion, parade style. Someone had located a discarded bugle of some kind. With the flag waving at the head of the parade and the bugle blaring, we marched out as proud Americans and Englishmen, conquerors, and survivors - a victory parade which ended at the ferry dock.

We boarded the ferry to Onomichi where a train waited to take us to Yokahama. At the time we did not know who arranged the logistics[39]. Aboard also were a

---

[39]In 1985, John Olson, then Col. retired, contacted me at my home. He had been trying to locate members of the Air Force crew he had arranged to liberate. (We soon learned we were living within five miles of each other.) I asked him to describe how he remembered our crew. He replied, "From the bow of the ferry traveling from Mukaishima to Onomichi you were flying the biggest American flag I have ever seen and playing loudly some kind of bugle. It looked like Washington crossing the Delaware." I replied, "Did any other repatriated outfits exhibit a flag?" He said, "No." Each confirmed the episode that took place.

number of Japanese guards and officers slated to be tried for war crimes and atrocities to prisoners. One of the officers, nicknamed Frog Eyes because of his looks, was also taken on the train. They now became our prisoners. The men in our P.O.W. camp had no love for the Japanese guards and officers. In fact, they hated them, and were pleased they would be tried as war criminals.

As the train passed through Osaka I saw some of the destruction rendered to this city as a result of the Keller crew's three bombing missions June 1, 7, and 15.

During our ride to Yokahama, as we passed each train station, we threw candies to the children and enjoyed watching them scramble for the goodies.

As the train slowly pulled into the Yokahama station, a U.S. military band decked out in their finest uniforms played patriotic music. I cried and was proud to show my emotions. I believe others felt the same, for not a dry eye could be seen. It was a spectacular event to behold as Gen. Robert Eichelberger greeted each P.O.W. with a welcome home handshake while the stirring music played on and on. What a thrilling moment! It will live in my memory forever. Many of the P.O.W.s looked like they could hardly walk, but they proudly presented themselves with a snappy salute.

We were then separated by branches of service and taken to an airplane hanger just off the runway at the Yokahama airport. In addition to the Americans there were Australians, New Zealanders, and British servicemen, now ex-P.O.W.s. We removed our worn out

---

Olson was not sure until we focused in on the flag. We became close buddies and played golf on a regular basis until he moved to San Antonio, Texas.

Olson graduated from the military academy (U.S. Army) at West Point in 1938. His first assignment sent him to the Philippines. A week before he was to return to the States, he was taken prisoner by the Japanese on Bataan and taken to Japan on the infamous hell ship and spent the entire war as a P.O.W. By the end of the war he could speak Japanese. MacArthur's forces asked if he would remain in Japan to assist in locating P.O.W. camps, scattered throughout Japan. He agreed and was responsible for locating our camp on Mukaishima. Olson arranged, through the Red Cross, to get trains and boat transportation and food enroute for the P.O.W.s.

and torn flight suits, stood there naked, while they deloused us with white powder and gave us fresh clothing. After a medical examination we were served a hot meal.

Our crew members were each assigned a cot and given clean bedding which was a treat from the uncomfortable rice mats. Thousands of P.O.W.s kept coming in, many in very bad shape. Most were extremely thin, unshaven and in ratty looking clothing.

Okinawa Typhoon

From Yokahama, our crew was flown to Okinawa on September 14. Others were flown or taken by ship to the Philippines or other ports to begin their trip back home. Our trip to Okinawa took place without incident, but as we attempted to leave Okinawa by plane for Iwo Jima, our flight had to be abruptly canceled as we headed down the runway. We were informed as we deplaned of an impending typhoon which turned out to be a devastating storm. I could not believe how violent a storm could be. The Navy put all of its ships to sea, but even with this precaution many ships and lives were lost. Had the atomic bomb not been dropped, it is possible this infamous typhoon might have caught the invasion fleet at sea, repeating the Kamikaze Divine Wind that destroyed Kublai Kahn's fleet 600 years earlier.

That night our tent was no match for the fury of the wind, so our crew rode out the storm by joining others to weigh down a Quonset hut we located nearby. As people joined us we hoped their added weight would help keep us on the ground, other service personnel went to the hills to sleep in burial caves.

The following day the storm continued and during breakfast the entire mess hall blew away right over our heads. All that remained, was a very large refrigerator, which furnished some protection from the driving wind and rain. We finished our meal huddled together behind the refrigerator, while watching the mess hall tumbling over and over, until it was completely destroyed. We sustained no injuries but were all shaken by the experience.

Finally, after breakfast, we got word we could leave. Our plane took off, stopping at our favorite filling station, Iwo Jima, to refuel and then on to Guam. There, we were hospitalized, treated for malnutrition, infections, and salt water sores and fed.

During our stay on Guam my wife received a phone call from a Philadelphia paper on September 18 telling her the good news that we had been repatriated.

The Red Cross on Guam was extremely helpful by arranging for us to send telegrams home. This was my first contact with Lucille. I had missed her so much and worried more about how she felt, than myself.

While at Guam we made application to the Caterpillar club (for parachuting) and the Goldfish club (for drifting in life rafts), and became members of both clubs. The requirements were pretty stiff.

One of our favorite sports during our relaxation periods was to throw coconuts under the dual wheel of passing trucks in order to break them open and eat the meat.

After spending six days on Guam, eating great meals and relaxing with wonderful people, we left on September 23, 1945, for the States stopping in Hawaii for two nights, with refueling at Kwajalein and Johnston Island along the way to Hawaii.

Debriefing

During our brief stay in Hawaii in addition to the debriefing meetings, we met with officers of the Navy about our drifting in the ocean and their attempts to rescue us.

We knew about the Air Sea Rescue procedure and had never doubted that we would be picked up, but it was at this meeting that we learned from the naval officers that the submarines could not come into the area where we were drifting because it was classified as restricted due to previous mining operations. We wondered, "Could we perhaps have sowed some of those mines?"

At the debriefing and talks with the navy personnel we learned about the intensive Air Sea rescue effort that had been made to locate us and their disappointment. Here we also learned that when Tulloch and Nelson crews reached Okinawa they had reported our coordinates to the Air Sea Rescue operation and desperately pleaded for permission to refuel and return to help us, but were informed that the air sea rescue would do this job and would locate us. Tulloch and Nelson were ordered to return to Tinian, but their actions had put into motion the forces of the Air Sea Rescue contingency[40].

Letterman General Hospital

Upon arrival in San Francisco on September 25, 1945, we went directly to the hospital. As hospitals go, the place was very nice. We were treated as somebody special. They put us two to a room, with meals served in a dining room for officers, with linen table cloth and napkins. Since we were underweight, they did their best to feed us well, the food was excellent.

As in all hospitals, the first thing they did was give us a complete physical examination. I mean complete, from head to toe. When it came time for urine exams Gene Correll always asked me to fill his bottle, he was afraid with his drinking he might not pass. He was lucky mine was okay. He did not want anything to delay his going home.

Immediately the Red Cross provided phone calls to our loved ones. Lucille and I had a lovely chat. We were so happy to be reunited by phone. In addition to hearing my voice, she was happy to hear about my promotion to Captain. I followed up my call with a letter outlining my experiences, told her all the P.O.W.s got a promotion (the hard way). I was proud of my railroad tracks.

We spent a lot of time recuperating and when not being treated or examined, we sat on a stone wall overlooking the Golden Gate Bridge and the bay, as we talked about our experiences and how lucky we had been, and about going home and making babies. In the

---

[40]See Appendix I page 173.

evening the lights from the bridge reflecting on the water gave us comfort.

The hospital arranged to take all of us to a college football game, doing their best to entertain us, and helping us to forget our experiences.

Homeward Bound

My orders finally came to return home on October 8, 1945. In those days it was very difficult to get train transportation with all of the troops coming home. It was out of the question to secure a plane ticket for Lucille to come to San Francisco. In fact, it never entered our minds that she should come there, it was just assumed that I would come home instead. None of the other crewmen brought their families there either. It was unheard of, in those days, to spend all that money, even if a ticket could be had.

The hospital transportation department arranged for me to have a private sleeping compartment, real style. Dressed in my newly tailored Eisenhower jacket with pink pants, so called because of their pink tint as opposed to the khaki color, pink hat and my captain bars, medals and ribbons I boarded the train for Philly, with a stop at Fort Wayne, Indiana, to visit with George Keller's parents. I had been selected for this very difficult assignment since I was the highest ranking officer on the crew. I wanted to go not only because it was my duty, but because I wanted to explain to his parents just how the events took place. It was a very emotional visit for all of us. I tried my best to comfort them. I did not want to raise their hope too high that he would be found but on the other hand, I did not want to give them false hope. I knew in my heart full well that he was dead but could not express it to them. It became a sad day, a depressing one as I left his grieving parents. As I sat in the train I asked, "What else could I have done?" I was not sure I had told them that their son was a hero.

Lucille and my parents were waiting on the train platform as the train pulled into the station. Lucille jumped all over me in excitement as I stepped off. We greeted each other with a squeeze that lasted until we just had to take another breath. They, Lucille and my parents, all talked at the same time with all sorts of questions.

My three brothers had returned from their service in Europe. Two of them married immediately.

Other servicemen were returning daily at a rapid rate so there were no parades or large parties. Everyone seemed to have a family member returning. My returning was no big deal except to Lucille. We had a lot of loving to catch up on.

The Air Force sent me for R&R in Florida for two weeks along with Lucille and my mother.

On March 12, 1946, I was separated from the service at Greensboro, and took up the business of selling insurance and raising a family.

In 1982 I was contacted by Gary DeWalt, a professional producer of documentary films, who was interested in making a film about our crew and the crew of the Lonesome Lady.

CHAPTER 13

Reunion With Fukui

His Story/August 7, 1983
    The day following my visit to Peace Park with Fukui's address in hand, my wife and I took (in order) the subway, a train from Kyoto to Ikachi, Yanai City, Yamaguchi, Pref, then by taxi to Lt. Fukui's home. We found it to be of unpretentious design by U.S. standards and located near a new highway just outside the city limits. I did not know what to expect since our last meeting had been 38 years ago.
    Years after the end of WWII, Lt. Nobuichi Fukui made contact with me by forwarding various objects crafted in wood in an attempt to create a market in the U.S. for Japanese goods through me. He introduced himself as the Japanese officer who contacted us while we were P.O.W.s in Hiroshima. Prior to this, we had no idea as to who he was or how to contact him. All that I knew was that it appeared he had saved our lives. Future correspondence with him confirmed this. He also sent the names and address of his Christian parents. Agnes Bartlett, the daughter of Samuel Bartlett writes;

> Dear Mr. Ross,   January 26, 1984
>   Zip code or not zip code your welcome letter arrived this morning, with a long awaited version of Tank's story of his contribution to the followers of Peace. The Box number was a bit off, but a small town post office is very helpful.

My association with Tank (Fukui) began in 1924 when the Exclusion Bill was passed in the U.S.A. It was a very hot July night in Kyoto. My mother had retired and my father was out of town. The cook and other help had gone to the movies, and I was 13, the "door-welcomer." I heard the tramp of many feet. Our consulate had warned us to stay off the streets lest there be hot heads (as in China) who might create an international incident. There was a knock on the front door; I opened it, as the daughter of the house to welcome the "guests." There was no returned bow. Led by a grim, square shouldered Doshisha-uniformed university student, a group of about 20 similar people marched into our living room. Their leader "Tank" Fukui grimly asked for my father.

I replied he was out of town. He then said, "Your mother will serve instead. We will talk to her." I ran upstairs, told my mother what was waiting downstairs. She ordered me to hide the Samurai swords (gifts to my parents from newly baptized Christians of a previous mission "field") and a horse pistol my four brothers had used for target practice. I did so, and she came down to welcome the "visitors" who were still grimly standing. Tank spoke on behalf of the students:

"Today your country has slapped our country in the face. There may be hot heads who would seek reprisal by annoying you. We are here to inform you that if one hair of your head is harmed it will be over our dead bodies. GOOD

NIGHT." And away they marched, led by "Tank."

As a "Missionary" brat it was fun to have the Japanese student "Big Brothers" coming in and out of the house for English practice and group singing. As the youngest of a family with four brothers separated from them by the Pacific Ocean, it was fun to be able to pass the cakes and tea after the Bible classes in the parlor. Tank was with a group that were able to take a rapid tour of the U.S.A. back then. My parents did the "Missionarying." I was just "Kid Sister" to the "Wild Rovers", and nice Big Brothers they were. It's hard to realize that it was 60 years ago!

My grandparents went out in 1872. My mother was the first "white baby" born in Osaka. I was born in Kyoto, and my four brothers were all born in Japan. My father was a "student volunteer" going from Dartmouth college to Japan to teach in 1887. Fifty years later, he died in Norwich, after he and my mother retired from the mission fields.

Thank you again for including me in your circle of Tanks' admirers.
        Signed
        Agnes V. Bartlett
        Daughter of Samuel Bartlett

I continued to be in touch with him and the Bartletts, who confirmed that they were indeed his Christian parents.

My purpose in wanting to meet him was two fold; one, I wanted to hear his story and to meet him again, and two., I wanted to assist DeWalt in the making of the documentary and to introduce him to Lt. Fukui. Fukui would become the key figure in bringing together this story.

It became very important that my meeting with him be cordial so that he would accept my invitation to participate in the filming the following day[41].

Fukui met us warmly at his door and invited us into his living area, a room of simple furnishings. He said, "Here, take these western style chairs, they will be more comfortable." He sat on the floor Japanese style, dressed very casually in trousers and without a dress shirt over his underwear. A tag still attached to his trousers told us they were newly purchased.

His wife Mariko, also a Christian, had met with an accident in 1982 and had been hospitalized since.

Fukui said, "After the war I became president of a local co-op where I introduced the concept of raising kiwis, after realizing that since New Zealand had the opposite seasons from Japan there would be a market for their fruit. MacArthur had divided the large tracks of land into small parcels, including my father's."

During his retirement years, he raised Bonsai trees, as many as 1,000. He continued to raise kiwi fruit and serve as President of the co-op.

Although I did not really know how to act, Fukui put us at ease. It became a pleasant and cordial meeting with stories about how I had informed General MacArthur's staff that they should look him up and treat him as one whom they could trust.

He laughed about the fact that they were expecting an American Christian since I told them he had Christian parents in the U.S. It became a big joke to him. Our conversation lasted over four hours reminiscing our meeting of 17 Aug 1945 and his eyewitness accounts of those days. He especially wanted to talk and tell about how 23 American P.O.W.s had died in Hiroshima as a result of their camp being destroyed as it became

---

[41]The documentary film "Genbaku Shi/Killed by the Atomic Bomb" was copywrited in 1985 for public television by Public Media of Santa Fe, New Mexico.

engulfed in flames created by the blast of the atomic bomb.

During our visit he invited us to remain overnight, he wanted to visit more. It became obvious he welcomed our visit and showed disappointment when we advised him that we were not prepared to stay overnight and could not change our plane schedule.

As we visited, he clapped his hands together and with that a woman entered the room on her knees and bowing from the waist. She wore a traditional kimono. He asked her to serve us some refreshments. After taking our order she backed out, still on her knees. Shortly thereafter she returned on her knees, with ice cream and cold tea.

I could not help thinking as we sat there together, "Here we were having a warm friendly conversation sharing war stories after having been enemies 38 years ago." I felt good about the meeting and that his story would be captured on film and become part of the documentary film and take its place in history.

During our visit he told us that as a Christian he had the urge to visit our crew. Although he had orders to arrange for our execution he wanted to secure safe passage for us.

He revealed the following story to us, which I had no knowledge.

Fukui's Story

"I was on my way home to Hiroshima on August 6, 1945, when I saw a flashing inside of the train station and heard a very loud explosion. It became so loud I thought a plane had crashed into a tank. It made a loud Boom! I had no idea as to the magnitude of the explosion until the train entered the city. I said to a friend, "What is the matter?" " It maybe a Japanese tank broken by a bomb from an airplane," he replied. Fukui continued, "Small fires broke out all over the city. I had an excellent understanding of the English language, and I had heard the broadcasts from the U.S. warning Japan about the bomb and its radiation. But I could not get the ear of the authorities."

He explained further; "According to international prisoner treaty signed by Japanese delegates that it was the responsibility of the Japanese to show P.O.W.s sign boards, letters on the roof of P.O.W. camps identifying their location, so U.S. aviators could avoid dropping bombs on P.O.W.s"

Fukui's stated "P.O.W. camps were not being identified." His statements are confirmed by the authors Gordon Thomas and Max Morgan Witts in their book <u>Enola Gay</u> when they explain that one of the reasons Hiroshima was selected for the first dropping of the atomic bomb, was that there was no evidence of the presence of a P.O.W. camp within the city. He went on, "For the lack of paint, no signs were on the P.O.W. camps in Hiroshima, and that 23 American P.O.W.s were killed by the atomic bomb." He kept stressing 23 Americans died.

"I will continue to my death to have the names of the 23 American P.O.W.s killed by the atomic bomb, be included in the Peace Park memorial in Hiroshima." he said.

As Fukui talked about the signs on the P.O.W. camp, my mind flashed back to our arrival at our P.O.W. camp were we permitted to paint on our roof Circle X 23 Crew Here on our roof.

He continued, "When I heard about the 10 aviators being held in a field near the Hiroshima train station waiting to be executed, I felt I needed to help them. My colonel said to me 'Do with them as you wish.'"

"Kill! Kill them! They are of no use to us now!"

Fukui said, "I successfully argued my case for safe passage for the American P.O.W.s." As he spoke I thought, "This was a bold position, in those days, for a Japanese lieutenant to take against a colonel in the Japanese army." Fukui continued, "My colonel understood my advice. Reversing his original decision to execute you," he told me, "I could get a military staff order regarding U.S. prisoners to prepare food and careful transportation with these powerful documents." "Luck has been with us again."

Fukui talked about his recent magazine article entitled "Secret Story of Hiroshima Atomic Bomb 38 Years Ago." (Dated 30 June 1983)[42].

Fukui's Article

"Twenty-three U.S. prisoners were dead by atomic bomb.

Several hundred thousand[43] lives were lost in a moment by atom bomb explosion 1945 and this case was repeated as for a rumor but their number and actual condition were not made clear."

Three persons, Mr. Norbuichi Fukui, Hirosh Yanagida and Kosuke Shishdo had Hiroshima experiences and after thirty years they met together there, and talked together about inviting N.H.K. editor Mr. Matsuo to listen to their reports.

As a result of the meeting, real creditable new history was made and it was perfectly different than U.S. history.

According to their conversation, it can be considered that some obscure points were made clear as for new historical data. Mr. K. Shishido presented these precious circumstances to famous magazine, Shukan Yomuri (weekly).

Consideration until today changes. The highest tragical atomic bomb explosion was exercised on 6 Aug. 1945 in Hiroshima (and later Nagasaki city). Today we recognize that thirty-eight years passed from that day while history is gradually altered year by year and tragically memory is going to forget.

One day at the beginning of February, I received a telephone call from N.H.K. Hiroshima branch (Mr. Matsuo editor) unexpectedly saying "<u>Do you know as a real fact 23 U.S. prisoners U.S. aviation in Hiroshima that were killed by the atomic bomb explosion?</u>" Mr.

---

[42]As translated from Japanese to English from weekly No. 33 (1983) from Shukan Yomiuri.

[43]Result of Hiroshima bomb was at least 130,000 and for Nagasaki a minimum of 35,000. Actually the death number would be 60,000, possibly 70,000. Source: <u>Day One</u> (Peter Wyden).

Hiroshi Yanagida who was a sergeant of Military Police station headquarters in Hiroshima made this case quite clear. Saying, "Therefore, N.M.K. desires to make a memorial schedule as to the atomic bomb explosion Aug 6th a Memorial day." He concluded to Mr. K. Shishido that N.H.K. hopes that he will cooperate with us joyfully. Memorial days will be established as for Hiroshima destroyed by atomic bomb explosion and its firing.

Indeed, I touched as to treatment of enemy prisoners but I thought carelessly that U.S. prisoners were four at least. Therefore, I was astonished that 23 prisoners were in Hiroshima instead of four. It is a remarkable case, including Hiroshima citizens about two hundred thousand were killed by the atom bomb explosion and the ensuing fires. It is natural that various rumors were spreading widely. About 200,000 citizens were killed by one bomb explosion and 23 U.S. sacrificers who also lost their lives but he is responsible to save by fair treatment. Mr. N. Fukui, first lieutenant calling soldier, M.P. headquarters, exceptionally escaped from the atomic bomb explosion (Brissette and Neal) and he had to treat U.S. prisoners (Keller Crew) as for an English interpreter called from Hitachi, Ltd. (a graduate of Doshisha University, Kyoto).

Under such condition and consideration we agreed to meet in Hiroshima. There we presented historical data together before N.H.K. editor Mr. Matsuo.

Mr. Matsuo[44] arranged history and made schedule to visit with camera man to U.S.A. such families of 23 U.S. prisoners who died by atomic bomb explosion and firing. As for exceptional case two among 23 prisoners Mr. Brissette (Norman Brissette) and Mr. Ralph Neal escaped from firing temporarily and carried to Military Policy station Ujima branch office.

Yamagida witness is as follows:

---

[44]Mr. Matsuo made a documentary film for Japanese television. His crew filmed Marty Zapf and me. Zapf's interview was included, but my interview was cut, because of my remarks about their attack on Pearl Harbor.

He is only one M.P. headquarters sergeant alive and was requested to present any piece of evidence of U.S. prisoners. He presented 23 U.S. prisoners individual dog tags which he found from ruins of fire of atomic bomb and requested they be presented after the war. Most of M.P. headquarters personnel were dead within one week.

U.S. officers accepted these metals[45] but U.S. government never replied about them. Nobody knows where these important metals are kept but God knows it! Mr. Yanagida is still alive and he can certificate this case any time but U.S. government give no answer because U.S. history will be corrected these wrong history of 23 prisoners.

Regarding N. Fukui's testimony, he was called by Lt. Col. Japanese Chugoku Military army staff and Fukui advised staff colonel to treat U.S. prisoners warmly based on International Prisoner Treaty (P.O.W.). signed by Japanese diplomatic negotiation under worst national conditions. The staff colonel understood Fukui's advice and Fukui could get military staff orders regarding U.S. prisoners to prepare food and careful transportation by these powerful document.

However, U.S. two prisoners Mr. Brissette and Mr. Neal could not be carried with ten U.S. Korean channel group prisoners (Keller Crew) by Japanese military doctor. After two days later, they were called by our Lord. The confession of these two patients to 10 U.S. Korean channel group whom Fukui carried to Ujima M.P. branch is still existed and the confession will be able to change U.S. wrong history if these ten Korean channel group appeal the fact as U.S. witness. U.S. families of 23 U.S. prisoners precious sacrificers will be favored with honorable fame by U.S. government. So long as I live I intend to encourage U.S. prisoners and I should like to cooperate with them to correct the U.S. wrong history.

---

[45] Dogtags were worn around the neck of each soldier identifying him and blood type.

These 23 precious sacrificers should brightly be favored as for priceless value toward eternal peace as same as 200,000 Hiroshima sacrificers. I herein stop to describe the more details because they are already published carefully through U.S. Kansas City Times including above two sacrificers Mr. Brissette and Mr. Neal on 20th Nov. 1975.

Various rumor and imagination once spread widely but I trust that truth will never be vanished and revives.

Japanese Premier Nakazone is coming to Hiroshima on 6th (August 1983) to attend the ceremony and will promise to accept their desire of 200,000 sacrificers and swear not to repeat war. Twenty-three U.S. prisoners names will be included finally. I believe heartily that our Lord will never put out the true fact."
                    Signed
                    Nobuichi Fukui

His second article dated July 29, 1983, follows[46];
"Regarding the atomic bomb in Hiroshima we should carefully study its historical fact bearing on trust which is really recognized by Our Lord.

U.S. Government once published about people in allies countries and the U.S. President declared the atomic bomb should result in freedom from world wars. Nobody can deny this statement.

General MacArthur could establish a new Japan without rejecting Japanese Emperor's system and Tokyo courts both could lead Japanese to international peace and now Japan can show highest peaceful purposes.

Japan should contribute toward real peace by abolishing the nuclear bomb. U.S.A. and Soviet Union can't exist together if one can defeat the enemy because atom bomb gas does not allow people and animals to live in either country.

Our Lord created the earth and educates people to maintain eternal peace but if special governments

---

[46]As translated from Japanese to English (per se).

betray God's will, a deserted earth will surely be realized.

Today I attached a description that should be carefully read. The atom bomb explosion truly killed twenty-three U.S. Army men in Hiroshima.

U.S. Government should correct its wrong history as quickly as possible. Also, the U.S. government should favor them with the highest fame managing unknown death which means missing soldier[47]."

Signed
Nobuichi Fukui

Upon the completion of our friendly conversation, he escorted us outside to show off his collection of bonsai trees, which numbered over a 1,000. I could hardly believe my eyes as we saw them. They were beautiful. I had never realized how many varieties there could be.

He insisted that he accompany us by taxi to the train station so he could stop on the way to show off his ranch, where he raised kiwi berries. He explained, "farms in Japan are called ranches." Having never seen kiwis grow before I was interested in the unique way they grew.

They were growing on a trellis of pipes about two inches in diameter that were curved from ground to ground in a half circle of about 15 feet. The pipes were fastened together to create a row of maybe one hundred feet. The plants were planted at the base of the pipes and the plant (or vine) grew up the pipe and over to the base on the other side, his plants were loaded with fruit. A person could walk under the arch formed by the pipes making it possible for a person to pick the fruit as it hung down from the branches.

---

[47] He also included the names and addresses of the Keller crew, Brissette and Neal.

As Lucille and I boarded the train Fukui handed to us copies of two magazine essays he wrote[48]. Having said our goodbyes, the train slowly pulled out of the Yanai station, then I suddenly realized that this might be the last time I would get to see this courageous man. It saddens me that we could not have spent more time with him.

During my ride back to Kyoto, I recalled the events leading up to this day. It, therefore, seemed important to me that I revisit the P.O.W. camp in which I had been interned.

---

[48]Separate reports to: 1)Dr. V Bartlett, P.O. Box 381, Norivichi, VT 05056. 2)Martin Sherwin, Historical Dept. of Princeton University (author of "Day One").

CHAPTER 14

Seeking P.O.W. Camp

The Trip

The next day I made a trip to my former P.O.W. camp with information and directions previously received from my radio operator, Marty Zapf, who had located the P.O.W. camp and visited with Lt. Fukui while he worked and lived as President of Burroughs of Japan. In addition, I enlisted help from the desk clerks at the hotel by showing them questions I had written in English and asked them to translate the question into Japanese. With this data on paper, I could stop passerbys and show them the questions in Japanese above my English words (many Japanese can speak English but not write or read English) so they could direct me in English. Such directions as, "What trains to take and departing times?" This became invaluable, and made my trip easier.

I departed early in the morning armed with my questions in hand and was off in quest of the P.O.W. camp. I knew it was on Mukaishima, opposite the town of Onomichi, but locating it became a challenge.

The day was hot and sticky with high humidity. My excitement heightened at being alone in a strange country which caused my pulse rate to accelerate. It became frightening at times, but as it turned out the people I stopped were friendly and helpful. As Franklin Roosevelt said, "There is nothing to fear but fear itself." Changing to and from trains, and subway trains, and locating the correct stations to get on and off became a challenge. The hardest part was making sure I was going in the correct direction. Boy, what a surprise was in store for me when I finally arrived at Onomichi. As I looked out from the train station, I saw what 38 years of time had done to the landscape, I couldn't believe my eyes, from my recollection of it being the small sleepy town I left in 1945. It was hard to recognize. A large bridge had been built from Onomichi to the island of Mukaishima, high enough to permit large ocean going vessels to sail under it. After locating a local map and securing a taxi driver who could somewhat understand me, we set off to the island by way of the new bridge.

I had, just eight months earlier, recovered from three angioplastics on my heart. The excitement of the day raised my pulse higher and higher as we came closer and closer to the island, but in spite of this I wanted to press on. My anxiety grew to a high pitch as we entered the completely built-up island. After the taxi driver dropped me off at the Ferry terminal, it became very difficult to orient myself. Looking first one way and then another, down one street and then another one at a time as they fanned out from the terminal, I could not recognize the area as I had known it. Finally, a young woman in her late teens came to my aid. Of course she was too young to have any knowledge of a P.O.W. camp, but she did secure another taxi and informed him of my quest. She talked with the driver a considerable amount of time, apparently trying to get him to understand.

The taxi driver drove as wild as those in New York City and Mexico. It became a hair-raising experience plus a frightening one. Very quickly I became aware that not only was I the only white person here, but the places he took me to were so far out of the way. Fear stepped in as he stopped several times to make phone calls, giving rise to how vulnerable I found myself with all the dead ends and his backing up and back in an effort to locate the camp. The longer it took the more frightened I became. Finally, with his last call, we drove to a building I could recognize from my memory and with the help of Zapf's photos. The driver dropped me off at the manager's office of a textile mill. Prior to WWII the building in which we were held prisoners had been a textile mill, after the war it reverted back to its original status.

The employees and management were delighted to see someone from the U.S. It became a great relief to me when they all gathered around a large table in their office and carried on an extensive conversation. Maybe they were just practicing their English skills on me, but I enjoyed their hospitality. They escorted me through the plant and tried their best to explain its function now and during the war. During our round table discussion in the manager's office, the conversation lead up to when I needed to leave to catch my train back to Kyoto. They brought out time tables and schedules and went on and on in Japanese and back to English. They were anxious for me to stay and talk, but finally they summoned a taxi and I started my trip back to my hotel. I crossed the bridge again and was dropped off at the train station.

I did the best I could to get some food to take aboard the train by using primarily sign language and was successful. I made my purchase and boarded the train. It became a day to remember, one that would be hard to express to another person.

As I ate my food during my train trip to Kyoto, I thought back to how it came about that our crew ended in a P.O.W. camp on Mukaishima.

The visit to the P.O.W. camp, seeing the hatred expressed in the exhibits in the museum, the feelings at the Peace Park, the demonstrations and having had the good fortune of seeing Lt. Fukui again, sparked me to re-appraise just how lucky our crew had been.

My thoughts returned to the first few minutes that took place after we landed in the ocean. We had one thing in mind as we assembled, "Would we be captured by the Japanese and taken P.O.W. and treated like we knew other P.O.W.'s had been treated on Bataan, Corregidor and China?"

Now after 38 years I could look back and become aware of the big picture, in which I had been blessed by "whom ever we worship."

The balance of our visit to Japan in 1983 was spent in sight seeing and learning about the Japanese culture. My wife and I visited Kyoto, an important religious center with 878 Buddhist temples and 82 shinto shrines and Japan's capital from A.D. 794 to 1868[49] with its Nijo castle built in 1500. The gardens of the temples are among the most beautiful in the world. The serenity of the raked gravel embracing large rocks had its calming effect on me after the events of the past few days.

I was proud of the United States for having the foresight to put Kyoto on the list of cities not to be bombed. We both enjoyed the fruits of that decision. It continues to be a beautiful city.

We even took in a James Bond 007 movie during our last night in Tokyo.

---

[49]Tokyo became the Eastern Capitol in 1868 under the Emperor Meiji.

EPILOGUE

From published stories in books like Enola Gay by Gordon Thomas and Max Morgan Witts, The Fall of Japan by Keith Wheeler, and editors from Time/Life books and The Fall of Japan by William Craig and from research done while filming the documentary "Killed By the Atomic Bomb" other P.O.W.s had been less fortunate than the Keller crew. In Craig's book The Fall of Japan, he tells of the horror of B-29 airmen being executed after becoming P.O.W.s.

The authors of "The Enola Gay" state that after WWII the U.S. interrogators, while interrogating Lt. Col. Oya[50], learned that 10 P.O.W.s had been murdered and their deaths passed on as having died in Hiroshima. Col. Oya claimed lost memory when asked for details.

Gary DeWalt, while making his documentary film, learned from various sources that it was true that the Japanese claimed deaths of P.O.W.s outside of Hiroshima had been listed as "killed by the atomic bomb." He also learned that some medical experiments on P.O.W.s were shown as having died in Hiroshima. All persons involved in these experiments have somehow mysteriously died.

Near Fukouka, Japan, located north of Nagasaki by about 100 miles, P.O.W.s were being systematically executed. Airmen from the Marianas were being held as P.O.W.s there. While Japanese officers conducted formal rites, eight B-29 airmen were executed on June 20, 1945.

Just one day after the atomic bomb had been dropped on Hiroshima Mr. Craig in his book "The Fall of Japan" tells of the execution on August 7, 1945, of eight B-29 crewmen in a field on a road from Fukuaoka to Aburayama. The P.O.W.s had been taken one or two at a time into a nearby woods, after leaving their truck, and after being stripped, were slaughtered.

---

[50]Quoted from the book Enola Gay.

Also in Nagasaki, from the book Enola Gay reference is made that there was a P.O.W. camp in Nagasaki at the time the second atomic bomb was dropped. Four Dutch prisoners died and three Dutchmen and one Englishman survived their injuries, while 38 others had to be treated for "after effects."

Again on August 11, 1945, the Japanese army officers sat down and planned to execute more American airmen who had been captured over the past three months. The Japanese officers had been aroused to do murder after hearing about the destruction of Nagasaki; they exposed their shiny silver swords, and using the cutting edge, beheaded the kneeling P.O.W.s, one by one, on and on until they came to the eighth airman. He was shot by an arrow and then executed in the same manner as his buddies.

Four days later, the 15th of August, 1945, while listening to the Emperor's speech of surrender, the officers at Fukuoka prepared a secret order to execute 16 American fliers because they knew too much about the fliers' deaths four days earlier and because they had bombed Japan. The P.O.W.s were taken by truck to the same location and with shouts of jubilation the guard conducted an orgy type of cutting up the airmen. After burying the unrecognizable bodies, they went back to their headquarters to burn all records of the P.O.W.s. The Japanese commander's girlfriend looked on, watching the execution (from The Fall of Japan by Craig). All of this took place while thousands of jubilant Americans celebrated the end of the war in cities all over the U.S.

Scenes like this took place in other parts of Japan and China where American flyers were being held by Japanese.

Also from The Fall of Japan by William Craig, is an account at the P.O.W. camp at Hoten in Manchuria. He states that over 1,700 P.O.W.s were being held, but were subsequently rescued by paratroopers.

It is easy for me to comprehend how a similar fate could just as well have happened to us, but thanks to efforts of many people I have come to realize how some events and happenings that took place were in our favor.

As a result of Fukui's action, we ultimately ended up safely (if a P.O.W. camp is safe) in Hiroshima camp #1 on the island of Mukaishima.

I wondered as I left Fukui, why he had such a great passion to have the names of the 23 Americans who died in Hiroshima included in the memorial book at Peace Park?

Was he disturbed, as a Christian and having received the love from the Bartlett family, as he witnessed the conditions in Java and China as to how they were treated by the Japanese soldiers? What did he think when he returned to his homeland and saw the destruction, especially Hiroshima? Did he feel obligated to help my crew when he heard that we were to be executed? I keep asking myself, "Why did he single out me and the Keller crew? Would I have done the same if the tables were reversed?"

APPENDIX A

The B-29 Superfortress

A standard B-29 crew consisted: a pilot called "aircraft commander," co-pilot called "pilot," bombardier, navigator, radar navigator, radio operator, flight engineer, central control gunner, left, right and tail gunners. A tunnel ran through the two bomb bays, connecting the front and rear cabins. Crew members could crawl through the tunnel to get to either cabin. It had four gun turrets, two above and two below carrying 12 caliber machine guns controlled from four locations, i.e. bombardier, central control, right, left gunners positions. The plane was the biggest and most complicated mass produced operation aircraft that had ever been built.

It carried almost as much fuel as a railroad tank car and its normal weight was one-seventh of a railroad locomotive, but four times its power. The B-29 was almost twice the weight and power of its predecessor, the B-17 (flying fortress) as follows:

	B-29	B-17
Length	99'	75'
Wingspan	141'	104'
Wing Area	1,739'	1,420'
Empty Weight	78,000 lbs	41,000 lbs
Max gross weight	135,000 "	64,500 "
Power	8,800 HP	4,800 HP

Its maximum payload (bombs) was 20,000 lbs for 2800 miles. Its tail fin (vertical stabilizer) stood 34' from ground to top.

The B-29 (powered by four R-3350 Wright Double Cyclone radial engines, each with 18 cylinders in twin banks swinging four blade propellers of 16' in diameter) had an operating range of 5830 miles round trip. Bombing runs from Tinian to mainland Japan were about 3000 miles and took about 14 hours on average to complete. The plane had a maximum speed of 365 MPH at an altitude of 31,000 feet, however due to the high jet streams over Japan the ground speed sometimes exceeded 450 MPH. The normal cruising speed was between 200 to 250 MPH. The B29 carried a load of either high explosives or incendiary bombs and on some missions it was equipped to carry naval mines, which were dropped by parachute from low altitudes of 5000 feet into shallow waters in and about harbors and shipping lanes. A typical bomb load was about 12,000 pounds on a mission of 3700 miles. Due to this high bomb load the plane was equipped with a tri-cycle landing gear each with two wheels. This plane was the first of its kind to use pressurized cabins, allowing crews to fly at a higher level out of the reach of fighter planes, and to offer more effectiveness. The B-29 was the first plane equipped with computer assisted remote controlled gun turrets and carried the latest in electronic equipment to include radar for navigation and bombing, with radar altimeters for long distance and precise navigation. It was the "State of the Art" - biggest, heaviest, and most complicated. It completed its first combat mission on June 5th, 1944 against Bangkok from its base in India.

  The B-29 had its first flight on September 21, 1942, and 3,965 planes were built during and shortly after WWII. The plane also saw combat during the Korean War (1950).

APPENDIX B

Nose Art

At first B-29s had no names or markings during most of the crew's training period in the United States according to psychologist Edwin Larson of State university of New York City college.

The names and nose art appeared when the planes were readied for combat. The members of crews were allowed only to have the names of someone's wife, or girlfriend on the fuselage near his station (position) in the plane, but shortly after arriving overseas however the planes blossomed with distinctive "nose art" and less conventional names.

Mr. Lawson flew with a B-29 squadron on Siapan and noted it was unusual for well known bombers like the <u>Enola Gay</u> named after the pilots mother (the B-29 that dropped the first atomic bomb in combat) to have individual names. 116 of the roughly 1,000 combat planes he analyzed he discovered that nearly half had sexual or suggestive names i.e. Suspine Sue, Adam's Eve and Teaser.

Other categories were cartoon and characters like (Flying Jackass); names of cities only (city of Los Angeles) and logo plus name (Kansas Farmer).

These distinctive names were morale boosters. It was a lot more fun and a lot more impressive for the air and ground crews to refer to their planes by name as in the case of the Keller crew who became known as the crew of the Sad Tomato or Nip Clipper.

Another reason for attaching the names to a piece of military machinery was one attempt to humanize a brutal war. By naming objects in his world man attempts to show possession and some form of control.

APPENDIX C

The 9th Bombardment Group's History

The oldest bombardment group in the United States Air Corps, reaches back through the 1st Bombardment Squadron days before WWI and the Mexican Campaign in 1916. It served in France in WWI and was demobilized July 21, 1919. In 1924 it was reconstituted. Transferred to the Panama Canal area in October 1940 flying patrols out of Trinidad which continued until October 1942 when it was transferred to Orlando, Florida, to participate in training and experimental projects. On April 12, 1944, the 9th Bombardment Group was transferred to McCook, Nebraska, to train in B-17 and in July they saw their first B-29. Overseas movement commenced in November 1944 and began its first combat mission in January 1945.

APPENDIX D

Mission	Plane#	Destination	Bomb Load	Date
				May
1	796	Tsuruga Bay	Mines	18
2	994	Fushika, Nigata	Mines	24-25
				June
3	796	Osaka Urban Area	Incendiary	1
4	561	Osaka Urban Area	"	7
5	561	Osaka Urban Area	"	15
6	285	City of Yokkaichi	"	11-18
7	285	Fukuoka	"	19-20
8	285	Moji Urban Area	"	28-29
				July
9	285	Ube Urban Area	"	1-2
10	512	Wakayama Urban Area	"	9-10
11	285	Tsuruga Urban Area	"	12-13
12	285	Choshi Industrail Urban	"	19-20
13	285	City of Tsu	"	24
14	285	Ujiyamada Urban Area	"	28-29
				August
No credit	285	Wagoya Urban Area	"	1-2
15	285	Maebashi Urban Area	"	5-6
16	12	Yawata Industrial Area (Bailed out of plane)	"	8

APPENDIX E

It has been estimated by persons in high authority that if there had been an invasion of the Empire of Japan, as many as 1,000,000 American lives would have been lost. The dropping of the two atomic bombs saved those lives. There continue to be arguments on both sides of the issue regarding its use, accepted by some, rejected by others. I happen to believe it was right and additionally perhaps gave cause for my life being spared.

Dr. Taro Takemi, former president of the Japan Medical Associates, believes that most Japanese agree that the atomic bombing of Japan saved the country from more war and massive starvation (Source: The Washington Post), but Edwin O. Reischauer, former U.S. Ambassador to Japan, doubts that most Japanese agree with Takemi, however, he does feel that it makes good sense. He thought it was a mistake at the time to drop the bomb but now agrees. (Source: The Washington Post). Takeshi Okita, a Hiroshima University professor, said Takemi's report was hardly acceptable in light of the number who were victims of the bomb (Source: The Washington Post). Reischauer, Ambassador from 1961 to 1966, feels that the Japanese military would have never let the people of Japan surrender, they would have continued fighting resulting in an absolute massacre and starvation, with many millions dying (Source: The Washington Post). General Curtis LeMay wrote, "That probably three million Japanese casualties were saved since an invasion was not necessary." (Quote from <u>B-29 Superfortress</u> by Turner Publishing Co.)

APPENDIX F

The left gunner from the Nelson crew gives us the following eyewitness report:

"Our plane (Nelson's crew) was in the formation behind the Nip Clipper (Keller crew) when it was hit and flames began showing from the right wing. We dropped out of formation to ward off any possible Japanese fighters. I was the left blister gunner and had a clear view of your plane as it was going down. As the flames kept spreading I wondered why your crew wasn't bailing out. I kept thinking that the gas tanks were going to explode any minute. When I finally saw the crew exiting the plane I felt a sigh of relief. I watched your crew bail out in a very orderly manner, as though they had been lined up and ready to go. I saw all of the parachutes open except for the last individual[51] who jumped. His parachute only had time to unfold when he hit the water and the plane appeared to land right on top of him.

"Our crew in addition to one other plane[52] continued to circle you off the coast of Japan. We dropped our emergency supplies to you as we circled.

"Someone in our crew mentioned a Japanese boat coming towards you which we strafed and it apparently decided to go back[53].

"We continued surveillance until fuel became a problem and we headed for

---

[51] George Keller, airplane commander.
[52] "Scotty" Tulloch's plane.
[53] Explains why we only saw one ship the first night adrift.

Okinawa and landed there. After several days we flew back to Tinian.

"We flew a carrier mission to Guam after the war ended, where we learned that you had survived and been repatriated.

"I felt a great sense of joy and relief that you had made it."
    Michael Poprik
    Sgt., Left Gunner, Nelson crew

APPENDIX G

Secret Report

The following report is recorded on microfilm on Page 39, Jacket number 24, frames 1102 to 1136; marked secret and released for public consummation; (9th Bombardment Group Document).

Thirty aircraft were airborne, 29 hit the primary target in three formations. Loading was; 500 pounds M17 indendiaries, 200 rounds of ammunition in upper and forward turrets and 500 rounds in the tail. Bombing was at 20,000 feet. Heavy anti-aircraft was meager but accurate with Keller's aircraft, which was lagging in the formation, mortally crippled. Six enemy aircraft sighted of which two Tonys made a coordinated attack on Nelson's aircraft. Nelson and Tulloch buddied Keller's aircraft until the crew bailed out, harassed Japanese fishing boats that were nearby, and landed at Okinawa to coordinate Air Sea Rescue efforts. U.S. submarines couldn't assist as the crew was located in mined waters. Keller was killed in the bail out. The remainder of the crew were possibly the last B-29 crews to become prisoners of war. (The aircraft lost was the Nip Clipper, serial number 42-24913. Three aircraft made emergency landings at Iwo Jima, two at Okinawa. One other crewman reportedly wounded but not named. End of Yawata report. Marked secret.

APPENDIX H

Walter Ross	Identification Bracelet
	2 Eversharp pencils
	1 watch
Stan Levine	High school ring
	Sunglasses
	Watch and wrist band
	Fountain pen
Carl Holden	Identification bracelet
	Automatic pencil
	Watch and band
	Ronson lighter

Later on during the interrogation at Iwakuni headquarters on August 15, 1945, the following items were taken from:

Eugene Correll	Wrist bracelet
	Watch and band
Martin Zapf	Wrist watch
	Sunglasses
	Pen and pencil set
Gerald Blake	Prayer book
	Sunglasses
	Pen
Robert Conley	Parker pen
	Wrist watch
	Sunglasses
Christus Nikitas	Wrist watch
	Parker 51 set
Shelly Fowler	Eversharp pencil
	Buluva 17 jewel
	Watch
	Watch fob
Traverse Harman	Shaeffer Pen

APPENDIX I

Report of Search
HEADQUARTERS NINTH BOMBARDMENT GROUP
Office of the Intelligence Officer
APO 336, c/o Postmaster
San Francisco, California

10 August 1945
SUBJECT: Air-Sea-Rescue Search
TO: 313th Wing Air-Sea-Search Office
ATTENTION: Eugene F. Shenefiel, Captain, Air Force

On August 8, 1945, at 1128 bombs were dropped from 20,600 feet by the 3rd Squadron of the Ninth Bomb Group formation as part of the Twentieth Air Force incendiary raid on the city of Yawata, Japan. B flight of this squadron, consisted of 33V lead flown by Lt. Tulloch, and 23V right swing, flown by Lt. Keller. Flak at this time was reported to be from heavy guns, intense and accurate, with bursts at altitude. Both 33V and 26V report minor flak damage in this area, while 32V flying in C flight also received minor damage.

It cannot be determined whether or not Lt. Keller's aircraft had been hit, although several scanners thought they had seen a flak burst before bombs away very close to his ship. Immediately after bombs away, Lt. Keller had difficulty in closing his bomb-bay doors and also had a stuck prop-governor from I.P. through his bomb run. He bombed a short distance behind the formation due to his engine over-heating. It was reported that immediately after bombs away two (2) Tonys attacked 23V from 4 o'clock high and sprayed the aircraft from wing tip to wing tip. No. 3 engine caught fire and as the formation started to make its right turn after the target area Lt. Keller turned off to the left, followed by Captain Tulloch and Lt. Nelson who peeled off to assist him.

Lt. Nelson assumed the communications for 23V and both 26V and 33V accompanied the wounded aircraft toward the northwest. It was apparent to Lt.

Keller that it was necessary to bail-out as soon as possible. They passed nearby Okino Island (34-15N 120-075) but were advised by Capt. Tulloch not to bail out there, as there was a lighthouse, some small boats, and some signs of activity on the Island. The bail-out was made over water at approximately 34N-23 130-09?

A log of the communications is attached as prepared by Major Hansen from the radio operator's interrogation and lots.

The crews of 26V and 33V saw 11 or 12 chutes open and remarked that the first was orange in color and the balance white, and there was a slight delay between the first and second chutes. Ten (10) men were soon counted in dinghies, and the dinghies were soon brought together. The sea was calm and quiet. 33V flew low over the liferafts while 26V flew high for protection. Captain Tulloch dropped a sustenance kit, Gibson girl, and eight one man dinghies, and continued to orbit the survivors. While circling 26V noticed a Chinese junk about ten miles east of the island, and which appeared to be on fire. 33V reported smoke in the area. It was decided that Lt. Nelson after orbiting for sometime, continue to Okinawa and get help. At about 1500K when Captain Tulloch no longer had gas enough to stay, a message was dropped to the survivors saying that gas was low and that help would be there as soon as possible. It is doubtful if the message was received. He flew low over the islands and strafed a steam launch near shore, so that it could not get out to the men.

26V had contacted with Crosstown 691 and gave him all information necessary, but the submarine said it would be unable to surface in that restricted area. Lt. Nelson also had contacted with aircraft on "G" channel and gave their numbers as 46 and 37. He gave them information in shackle (?) as to the distress and the location of the survivors and was answered correctly in voice. 37 was apparently near the island at the time, and reported that he saw a small fishing boat, that he thought to be the Chinese junk. This may have been the boat that Captain Tulloch strafed as 37 did not report that he saw the survivors.. 26V then continued on to Okinawa and on approaching was unable to contact "Glacier" tower, but did contact "Drake" tower shortly before landing. Lt. Nelson immediately after landing, contacted an ASR Office at Okinawa immediately, giving them full details. They did not acknowledge receipt of emergency message, but said that they had been told that there was a possibility of survivor in area designated by message "50 Candlelight 200", which was obviously not the position given..

33V enroute to Okinawa had contact with Crosstown 521 but that submarine was unable to get complete message on VHF, saying several times that their transmitter was cutting out. He landed at Okinawa at approximately 1815K. All effort was made to have ?????? sent out as soon as possible.

Air-Sea-Rescue reported to both men that a Flying Dutchman and PBM would be sent out early in the morning, accompanied by fighters to search the area. Both men asked to go along, either with their own aircraft or with their search planes, but were told that it would not be necessary.

James F. Munson
1st Lt. Air Force
Air-Sea-Rescue Officer

The following named officers and enlisted men failed to return from an attack on the Urban Area of Yawata on August 8, 1945, and are known to have bailed out approximately thirty (30) miles northwest of the target:

1st Lt. George F. Keller	0820765
2nd Lt. Carlton M. Holden	0836796
2nd Lt. Eugene V. Correll Jr.	02078937
1st Lt. Walter R. Ross	01323741
2nd Lt. Stanley H. Levine	02065876
T/Sgt. Shelby L. Fowler	20460703
Sgt. Martin L. Zapf	42104732
Sgt. Robert M. Conley	36946965

Sgt.   Gerald J. Blake   12238769
Sgt.   Travers Harman   33190601
Sgt.   Christine M. Nikitas   31389684

(Note: This report is retyped from Microfilm Roll B0067, Frames 1202 and 1203.) The material was marked "Secret."